365 DAILY PRAYERS AND DECLARATIONS FOR MEN

BroadStreet
PUBLISHING

BroadStreet Publishing Group, LLC.
Savage, Minnesota, USA
Broadstreetpublishing.com

365 DAILY PRAYERS AND DECLARATIONS FOR MEN

© 2022 by BroadStreet Publishing®

978-1-4245-6400-2
978-1-4245-6401-9 (eBook)

Devotional entries composed by Jared Winger.

Design and typesetting by Garborg Design Works | garborgdesign.com

Editorial services by Michelle Winger | literallyprecise.com

Printed in China.

22 23 24 25 26 27 28 7 6 5 4 3 2 1

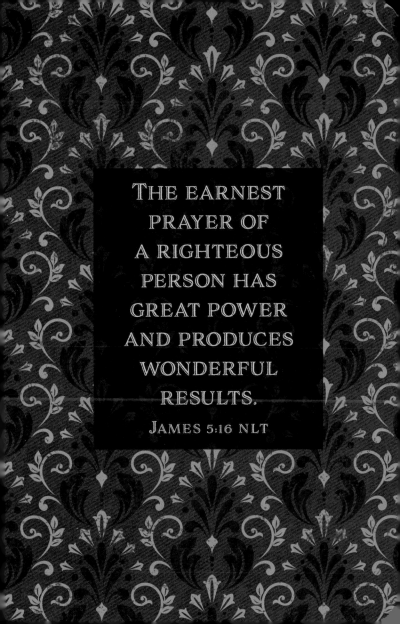

THE EARNEST
PRAYER OF
A RIGHTEOUS
PERSON HAS
GREAT POWER
AND PRODUCES
WONDERFUL
RESULTS.

JAMES 5:16 NLT

Introduction

"The earth and sky will wear out and fade away
before one word I speak loses its power
or fails to accomplish its purpose."

MATTHEW 24:35 TPT

This is one of the many promises God has spoken over you.
His promises are for every situation and for all time. They
reflect his character and confirm his purpose for your life.

This book of prayers and declarations will help you gain
confidence in the never-ending love and mercy of God.
When you need encouragement or a reminder of who God
is, turn to his Word and declare it over your situation. God's
Word is living and active and as relevant today as it was
when it was written.

As you reflect on these daily entries, grab hold of God's
promises, declare them over your life, and discover his
unlimited grace and strength.

JANUARY

The earnest prayer of a
righteous person has great
power and produces
wonderful results.

JAMES 5:16 NLT

The Delightful Way

What delight comes to the one
who follows God's ways!

PSALM 1:1 TPT

God, I want to delight in you. I want to know what it means to not have a desire to follow my own ways but find great joy in doing your will. Help me to see that your path is secure, your plan is good, and your desire for me is excellent. When I do, I know that I will find delight in you.

Help me not to look at others and envy them; help me to trust that even if my life is not in a good place, I can know you are working in me, for me, and to help me grow. I know you want me to be like Jesus and walk as he walked. He listened to you, and he knew your voice. I ask that you would help me to do the same.

Father, because of your good intentions for me, I will delight to do your will. I will place myself in your care and allow my heart to be undone by your goodness. You are faithful, your ways are perfect, and I can trust you. There is joy in knowing your ways.

Delivered

He delivered us from such a deadly peril,
and he will deliver us.
On him we have set our hope
that he will deliver us again.

2 CORINTHIANS 1:10 ESV

God, I thank you for your mercy. Though I do not deserve it, you have saved me from death. I ask that you would help me to understand what you have truly done for me in the midst of my busy life. I know at times I forget how much you have done.

I honestly don't feel like I face deadly peril often, but that is because I do not see as you do. Help me to see things as you see them. I pray that as I do, I would continue to place my hope in you. I don't want to hope in man, in governments, or in global changes. Help me to trust in you alone.

You are a mighty God. There is no one who stands above all others, who rules with authority and power like you do. You rule over life, death, and humanity. You rule over everything, and I will trust in your deliverance.

Strong Faith

If your faith remains strong, even while surrounded
by life's difficulties, you will continue to experience
the untold blessings of God! True happiness comes as
you pass the test with faith, and receive the victorious
crown of life promised to every lover of God!

JAMES 1:12 TPT

God, I pray that my faith remains strong and ask that I
would be remembered as a lover of you. I think that would
demonstrate to others how much, regardless of testing and
difficulty, I was able to stand steadfast in you.

I pray you would help me look forward to my resurrection in
you, and not be caught up in this life. Help me to keep my
perspective centered around your kingdom and not my own.

*Jesus, you are the faithful and strong one. I trust in the
victory that you have already accomplished. I know you are
steadfast, and I can trust in you. I will take time in the midst
of difficulty to intentionally trust in your goodness.*

Rescue

He has rescued us from the kingdom of darkness
and transferred us into the Kingdom of his dear Son.

COLOSSIANS 1:13 NLT

Father, sometimes I don't feel like being rescued; I want
you to leave me alone. But I know that you continue to
chase me down and show me how much I am steeped in
darkness, and I have lost my way. Thank you. Thank you for
saving me.

Thank you for showing me my sin and error and for helping
me to come to the light. I ask that you would continue to
soften my heart and draw me to your Son.

*God, you are the faithful one who does not relent. You are
a passionate pursuer of your people. You will not leave us
or forsake us. Even when we don't want to be chased, you
are there waiting. You are powerful and boundless. No one
stops you when you want to move. I believe in you, I believe
in your power, and I believe in your kingdom.*

Good Gifts

Every good action and every perfect gift is from God. These good gifts come down from the Creator of the sun, moon, and stars, who does not change like their shifting shadows.

JAMES 1:17 NCV

God, help me to trust in your goodness. I ask that you would give me your eyes to see things the way you do. Help me to have the vision of the world that you have, so I can see what you are doing and see your creation from your perspective.

Help me to know your steadfastness in the midst of the shifting shadows of life. I slip without your steady hand holding me firm, and I need to know that you are there for me.

You are wonderful, good, and faithful, Father. It is in you that I have confidence. I know your actions for me are intended to bless and create growth in me. I believe you do good things, and just as you created the heavens and the earth with amazing detail, you have the details of my life in mind.

Eternal Hope

The hope of eternal life, which God, who does not lie,
promised before the beginning of time.

TITUS 1:2 NIV

I thank you, God, for eternal life. You have given me
promises and you do not break them. I am so grateful to
know that there are better things to come and that despite
the troubles of this life, I will be with you in your kingdom.

I thank you also that you do not lie and that I have security
in you. I ask you to help me trust in who you are and not in
my own abilities.

*Father, you provide an inheritance for those who believe
and follow your ways. You are forever, and your promises
will not fail. You are truth and life, and in you I can find
peace and strength that I cannot find anywhere else. You
alone are my rock and my righteousness, and I believe that
you have stored up for me a good inheritance.*

Saying Yes

The yes to all of God's promises is in Christ,
and through Christ we say yes to the glory of God.

2 Corinthians 1:20 NCV

God, sometimes I find it hard to say yes to you. I don't find it hard to say yes to myself. I ask that you would give me strength to turn my focus from myself so I can pay attention to you. I find it difficult to do, but I know it is important for you to be glorified in my life, so please help me to say yes to you.

Thank you for your promises and thank you that I can trust in your Word. I love that what you say is true and what you do is faithfully loving. Help me to take this belief and trust in you enough to say yes.

Creator God, your glory and greatness are unmatched. You are good and your Word endures with supremacy. Your promises never fail because you are truthful and loving. You do not depend on man to provide because you are the ultimate provider. I trust in your provision.

Creative Qualities

Ever since the world was created, people have seen
the earth and sky. Through everything God made, they
can clearly see his invisible qualities—his eternal power
and divine nature. So they have no excuse for not
knowing God.

ROMANS 1:20 NLT

Father, I thank you for giving me sight. Thank you for the
beauty of your creation. It shows how wonderful and fun
you are. I want to be able to know you more and to take
time to contemplate your qualities seen in how you make
things.

I want my heart to be captivated by your creativity such
that I would be curious about your qualities. Help me to be
filled with awe and wonder at who you are and not so full
of myself that I am blinded to you.

*Your ways are amazing. Your beauty is demonstrated in
your creation. Your marvelous power is manifest in the
earth. You are worthy of my praise. My lips will speak of
your greatness. There is no one like you God; you are
unparalleled in person and incomparable in creativity.*

Joy Opportunity

When troubles of any kind come your way, consider it an opportunity for great joy. For you know that when your faith is tested, your endurance has a chance to grow.

JAMES 1:2-3 NLT

When trouble comes my way, God, I tend to run. I don't want to face it because I want my life to be full of interest, ease, and fun. But I know that life is not always like this, so I ask that you would help me to see trouble as an opportunity to embrace challenge.

Help me to grow in times of trouble instead of trying to avoid them. I want to know your joy and your fellowship when I face distress and worry.

God, you have endured more trouble than anyone on earth. You know what it means to demonstrate character in the face of change. You never ran away, you never gave up, and you never avoided. You are strong, faithful, enduring, and overcoming. I trust in your strength and joy when I am facing troubles of any kind.

No Fault

All glory to God, who is able to keep you from falling
away and will bring you with great joy into his glorious
presence without a single fault.

JUDE 1:24 NLT

Jesus, thank you for what you did on the cross so we could
be restored to the Father. Thank you for your sacrifice
to save me from my sin. You know how much my heart
wanders away from you.

Every day I struggle with failure, yet you continue to love
me and keep me. Who is there like you? I love and thank
you for presenting me with great joy. I thank you that
unlike humanity, you are not ashamed of us all; you are not
ashamed of me.

*Lord, you are able to keep me, you are able to hold me in
your hand despite my failings. Your faithfulness overcomes
my faithlessness. What an amazing God I serve! Despite
my shameful actions, you unashamedly present me to your
Father with great joy. You are so kind and loving.*

Wise Ways

The foolishness of God is wiser than human wisdom, and the weakness of God is stronger than human strength.

1 CORINTHIANS 1:25 NIV

Father, thank you that you are so wise. I pray that you would help me to rely on your wisdom and guidance rather than doing things in my own strength. Help me to have patience to wait upon you.

I tend to want to do things right away rather than wait on you. Help me to rest in your wise ways. Give me your strength to do the things you want and to put aside my desires that are not of you.

There is no one like you, God. There is none who has your understanding and wisdom. You hold the keys to life in your hands. Your ways are perfect, and your thoughts are pure. You alone know all things and give clarity to me when I need it. I rely upon you, God, for all wisdom and understanding. I trust even when I do not understand because your ways are right. I find peace in you alone.

What I Need

By his divine power, God has given us everything we
need for living a godly life. We have received all of
this by coming to know him, the one who called us to
himself by means of his marvelous glory and excellence.

2 PETER 1:3 NLT

Blessed are you, God, for all that you have given. I love that
you do not want me to be limited by anything. Help me to
see what you have provided, and to trust that when I do
not see what I need, you will deliver.

Help me to know you more, to draw closer to you, and to
be enamored by your glory and excellence. I want to be
at rest in knowing beyond doubt that you are everything,
and that because you created me, you know exactly what
I need.

*In you, God, I have everything I need. I can be content
because I know that you are good, you care, and you want
the best for me. I can rest in knowing your provision is
enough. Though I fail, you are faithful. You never run out of
resources to equip me for endurance and life.*

Generous Inheritance

> Blessed be the God and Father of our Lord Jesus Christ! According to his great mercy, he has caused us to be born again to a living hope through the resurrection of Jesus Christ from the dead, to an inheritance that is imperishable, undefiled, and unfading, kept in heaven for you.
>
> 1 PETER 1:3-4 ESV

Father, thank you for what promises I have in you. When I dwell upon your words, I find them to be living water to my parched soul. I pray that as I read your Word, it would melt my heart for you, and meld it to you.

Thank you for your mercy. Though I struggle each day, you cover me in your love and kindness. Thank you for life in you!

You are blessed, Father. Thank you for the vials of mercy poured out on my life. Thank you for giving me hope and promising resurrection. I will live with you forever! You not only give me eternal life, but also an inheritance and gifts that will never fade. You are a generous father.

Best Comfort

Praise be to the God and Father of our Lord Jesus Christ. God is the Father who is full of mercy and all comfort. He comforts us every time we have trouble, so when others have trouble, we can comfort them with the same comfort God gives us.

2 CORINTHIANS 1:3-4 NCV

Father, I so need your comfort. My soul is troubled by many things in this life. Relationships, money, and work all pull my life in troubling directions. Help me to find comfort in you and not in other things. I want relief from you like the feeling of coming home to a hot meal, and a warm home, on a cold, wet day.

I know I need help, but sometimes I busy myself with other things, so I don't feel it. Help me to rest in you, Father.

Your comfort is the best. You know me better than I know myself. You are merciful and kind. You are strong and wise. You speak words of life to me even when I do not hear. In any state I am in, I can come to you, and you will be with me.

Perfect Work

Let patience have its perfect work,
that you may be perfect and complete,
lacking nothing.

JAMES 1:4 NKJV

Father, I feel like patience escapes me easily. Why, when I need it the most, does it evade me? Help me to take time to trust in you. Help me to release control and let go of the perception that I have control. I need your help with this because it is why I become impatient.

Ironically, I lack the things I need to be patient and therefore perfect and complete. Help me to realize this and trust in you to do your work in me.

God, you are perfect and patient. You work into me the things I lack. I trust in your power to labor with me in developing patience. You are in control and have all knowledge and ability to remain so. There is no wavering in who you are, no wondering about your endurance. You are my serenity.

A Witness

We know, brothers and sisters loved by God, that he has chosen you, because our gospel came to you not simply with words but also with power, with the Holy Spirit and deep conviction. You know how we lived among you for your sake.

1 Thessalonians 1:4-5 niv

Father, thank you for those who have been a witness to me of your power and Spirit. I ask that you would help me to continue their testimony by living similarly. Help me to live by your Word and be convicted by it when I do not.

Help me to be an example to those who will follow my lead.

God, your gospel is powerful. Your Word does not return void. You have set an example that I want to follow and exemplify to others. You chose me to be in your family, to know the same power that resurrected Christ, and to be filled with your Spirit. Jesus you are my Savior, and your words are perfect for my instruction.

Faithful Light

This is the message we have heard from him and declare
to you: God is light; in him there is no darkness at all.

1 JOHN 1:5 NIV

God, I love that you bring light into my life. Sometimes I
shy away because of the darkness I have allowed myself to
stay in, but I love that you are like the sun brightly shining
after a dark stormy night.

Thank you for reaching out to me in my darkest hours
and redeeming me. Thank you for helping me to see the
dangers ahead, for lighting up my path, and showing me
the way. I need you to continue revealing the right path
and helping me follow you more closely.

*Father, you are my light in the darkness. You never tire, run
out, or break. You are the faithful light that shows me the
way. I can trust in your guidance. I know you want the best
for me, and you do not want me to stumble. I depend on you.*

Because of Love

Because of his love, God had already decided to make us his own children through Jesus Christ. That was what he wanted and what pleased him.

EPHESIANS 1:5 NCV

Father, I am humbled by your choice. Thank you for choosing to make me part of your family. Thank you that it was not an obligation, but it was for your pleasure. I am taken aback by your generous love that knows no bounds.

I ask that you would help me to demonstrate this same love to others. I want to reflect a joy in sacrificing for others. Help me to express your kindness and goodness, to strive to love others as well as you love me.

God, your love knows no constraints and fills every space to overflowing because you are love. You chose me because you are love. It was your pleasure to choose me not because of who I am but because you are love. You cannot be anything but loving. You are love.

Wise Counsel

If any of you needs wisdom, you should ask God for it.
He is generous to everyone and will give you wisdom
without criticizing you.

JAMES 1:5 NCV

I ask for your wisdom, God. Please help me to know
your ways. Every day I have decisions I need to make
that require discernment beyond my years. Help me to
be as perceptive as you are. Help me to rely upon your
knowledge and trust in your understanding.

Thank you that you that you do not withhold from me
because of who I am. Thank you for generously giving
what I need each day.

*Your judgments are perfect, Jesus. Your ways are without
fault. I trust in you to provide what I need. You do not
suppress me but give lavishly for my success in your ways.
You are faithful in what you give and in listening to my
prayers. I will read your Word and accept the guidance of
the Holy Spirit who is my wise counselor.*

Aware of Me

"Before I formed you in the womb I knew you,
before you were born I set you apart."

JEREMIAH 1:5 NIV

Father, it is hard for me to allow this Scripture to truly penetrate my heart. How are you cognizant of me, and even more so, before I was born? I pray this would help me to know how secure I am in you. Help me to know that there is no way I can ever be taken from you or lose my relationship because of you.

I need to know this deep in my heart, so I always remain faithful to you. I ask that the knowledge of how much you are aware of me will solidify my commitment to you. Help me to be wholeheartedly devoted to you.

God, your knowledge of me knows no bounds. You are not limited in understanding or capacity to comprehend. You are magnificent in how you handle me. You are full of confidence in the best way forward for my life, and I can trust that you will do in me what you desire.

Completed Work

I am sure of this, that he who began a good work in you
will bring it to completion at the day of Jesus Christ.

PHILIPPIANS 1:6 ESV

Thank you, God, that you are sure of what you will do in
me. I am not always so confident. I pray you would help me
to trust the work you are completing. I feel like I am slow to
learn and fail so often which makes me wonder about the
work you are accomplishing.

Help me to mature and become more like your Son, Jesus.
I want to do your will, but I struggle so much with my own
desires. Help me to see the forest through the trees. I don't
want to be so caught up in my day-to-day struggles and
not see how you are moving me forward.

*You are at work in my life, God. You are a good father,
a strong shepherd, a loving God. I trust that you will
complete your work in me and that when Christ appears,
he will be pleased with me. By your grace, I will be ready
for that day.*

Place in Time

Be truly glad! There is wonderful joy ahead. You love him even though you have never seen him. Though you do not see him now, you trust him; and you rejoice with a glorious, inexpressible joy.

1 PETER 1:6, 8-9 NLT

Jesus, I want to trust you, but I struggle with dependence upon myself. I do love you and want to love you more, so I ask that you would give me strength and greater will to do that.

Help me to understand my place in time, that life is short, and that I do not live for this age. My joy and fervor in this life is because I have a future and a hope in you. My petition before you today is that my life would evidence an eternal perspective. Help me to place my confidence in you alone.

God, you are worthy of wonder. You are loyal to your Word and trustworthy. You have stored up for me great treasures and have promised me life everlasting. I do not put my hope in this life, but I will trust in you to prepare me and have me ready for eternity with you.

Pure Light

If we keep living in the pure light that surrounds him,
we share unbroken fellowship with one another,
and the blood of Jesus, his Son,
continually cleanses us from all sin.

1 John 1:7 tpt

Jesus, thank you for cleansing me from all of my sin and not just some of it. Help me to walk in the light as you did when you walked the earth.

I know that I do not see all of my brokenness and wrongdoing. I may even feel right and have done wrong without knowing. I ask that you would show me; help me to repent and walk in the light. Reveal the things that I do not see so I can be pleasing to you. I love being with you, Jesus.

Savior, the cross was enough to cover my sin, the sin of the world, and all the sin in the future. You have brought me into the light, and I thank you for showing me how to live. You provide all that I need to have fellowship with you.

Enduring Faith

These trials will show that your faith is genuine. It is being tested as fire tests and purifies gold—though your faith is far more precious than mere gold. So when your faith remains strong through many trials, it will bring you much praise and glory and honor on the day when Jesus Christ is revealed to the whole world.

1 PETER 1:7 NLT

Father, I know that trouble in my life can be used for your glory, and I ask that you would help me to see what you are doing in me and not become discouraged. Help me to be strong in my faith, to endure, and to learn what it means to praise you in the midst of trial.

It is easy for me to respond negatively when I am distressed, and I pray that you would encourage me. Remind me to live for eternity and not for this moment.

You will be glorified in me, Jesus. You will be honored by my life because you have caused me to be strengthened in times of trouble. It is your name that will be lifted up because of my victory over sin and death. You make my faith endure.

No Fear

God gave us a spirit not of fear
but of power and love and self-control.

2 TIMOTHY 1:7 ESV

Father, I desire to know your Holy Spirit on a level that enables me to have self-control. I ask that you would take me deeper into you, so I would not fear the unknown.

I want to know the power of your resurrection in my life, so please pour out your Spirit on me. I want to love better and when I interact with others, I desire that they would see your Spirit in me. Thank you that you have given me your assurance and I can trust you.

You are strong and mighty. There is no one like you, Jesus. You are my fortress and my shield. In you I have no fear, but am filled with your love, power, and the ability to be controlled. You are my strength, and I will trust in you. You have given me what I need to live this life in faith and to endure all things until you return. I am secure in you.

Merciful Gift

He is so rich in kindness and grace
that he purchased our freedom
with the blood of his Son and forgave our sins.

Ephesians 1:7 NLT

Father, I want to understand the freedom that you have given in a greater measure. I pray over my heart that the blood of Christ would renew and change me to be more like your Son. I pray that the liberty from sin you provided, Jesus, would allow me to walk in kindness and grace.

Help me to show mercy and goodness to others because of what you have done in me. Thank you for paying for my sin. I am so humbled that you would do this for mankind, and that you chose me to be a recipient of your merciful and generous gift.

It is your kindness that has softened my heart. Your mercy allows me to return to you in humility, and your forgiveness gives me life. Thank you, Jesus, for your lavish love for me. You have given me freedom to live for you and I choose to follow you. I give you my life in return for your sacrifice.

Troubled Times

The LORD is good,
a refuge in times of trouble.
He cares for those who trust in him.

NAHUM 1:7 NIV

Lord, you are good to me. I want to take refuge in you. I want my heart to be rested in knowing you. You care so much for me, and no matter what trouble I face, you will be with me. Help me to see how you care for me even when I feel overwhelmed.

Show me what you are doing. There are things I face in life that I feel never leave me—troubles of the soul. I ask that you would give me rest from these. That you would bring me comfort and be my helper.

There is no one else for me, Jesus. You have what I need to get through troubled times. I trust in your ability to bring me comfort and strength. I believe that you care for me. You are interested in my life. You know how many hairs are on my head. I can rest in you.

Powerful God

"You will receive power
when the Holy Spirit comes on you."

ACTS 1:8 NIV

God, I need you to show up in power. I see those around
me who are sick, who are hurting, and who need the help
of a powerful God. I also need that from you. I am not sure
what you want besides a willing vessel to work with. I want
you to know I am willing.

Fill my heart so I am not distracted by any other thing. I
ask that you would purify me and help my devotion to you,
so that the Holy Spirit is comfortable resting upon me. I
know you long for a holy people to arise, a people who are
set apart for you. Help me to be included, God. Do not let
your Holy Spirit pass me by!

*God, you are mighty. You are holy. There is no one like you.
There is none with your wisdom, insight, magnificence, and
splendor. I long for the demonstration of your greatness in
the earth. You will arise as the mighty one, radiating your
glory across this broken planet with great supremacy. You
are King Jesus!*

Speak Boldly

"Don't be afraid of the people,
for I will be with you and will protect you.
I, the LORD, have spoken!"

JEREMIAH 1:8 NLT

Father, I find myself fearing man more than I should. There is so much you have given me, and so much you have promised me, yet I still fear what man may do to me. Help me to be like your Son, who fully trusted you.

I want to know in my heart that I do not need to fear. I want my faith to be strong enough that I can state your Word boldly and not worry about what people will think, or what they will say or do. I need you to fill me with your Spirit, so I am overflowing with truth and love.

You are great, God. There is no fear in you. You are my confidence, and you prosper me. You give me life and fill me with the joy that overcomes my apprehension. In you, I am strong and self-assured. You will make me bold to speak the truth with boundless love.

The Return

"I am the Alpha and the Omega," says the LORD God,
"who is, and who was, and who is to come,
the Almighty."

REVELATION 1:8 NIV

Lord, I am excited to think about your return. I know you
started the world to have a people of your own, and I
thank you for choosing me as one of them! I pray you
would come back soon, Jesus. I want you to establish your
kingdom on this earth in my lifetime. I want you to finish
sooner rather than later as I am weary of this world and
what it is doing to people.

Thank you for your mercy, but I ask for your might. The
time for mercy is ending, and we need the suffering and
sin of this life to end. We need the mighty warrior king to
claim his throne.

*God, you are the King of kings and Lord of lords. You will
come back and make all things right. The earth will groan
no longer but rejoice with the return of the Almighty. You
are going to dwell with your people on a new earth, and I
will be filled with joy, love, and peace, forever!*

Full Vial

If we confess our sins,
He is faithful and just to forgive us our sins
and to cleanse us from all unrighteousness.

1 John 1:9 nkjv

Thank you, Jesus, that you don't just cleanse me from one sin, but you cleanse me from all of it. I have sins that I don't even know about. Things that offend your holiness. Thank you that you sacrificed your life to make me righteous before God.

Help me to be sensitive to your Spirit so I would mature in my character and life. I want to stand before you on that day and see that I am pleasing to you. Please help me to have a soft heart and not allow recurring sin to turn me away from you. Help me to remain humble and admit when I am wrong.

I love your faithfulness, God. I am impressed by your unfailing love. You have poured out grace and mercy and I am a full vial, a clean vessel ready to be used for your purposes. You are right in your decision to forgive me because of your eternal and encompassing sacrifice. You are faithful and just.

FEBRUARY

Look to the LORD
and his strength;
seek his face always.

1 CHRONICLES 16:11 NIV

Wherever You Go

"Have I not commanded you?
Be strong and courageous.
Do not be afraid; do not be discouraged,
for the LORD your God will be with you
wherever you go."

JOSHUA 1:9 NIV

Father, thank you for your encouragement to be full of fervor for you. I want to be excited to serve you and be bold in doing so. Like Joshua, I want to go to where you take me with strong faith, and I need you to encourage my heart when I am lacking.

When I am struggling, please bring these words back to me so I can recollect your faithfulness to those who have gone before me. In my times of discouragement, be the voice that I need, spurring me on to overcome by the blood of the Lamb, and the word of your testimony. Let me be a living sacrifice and not shrink away from pain or even death.

God, I will be brave facing my foes. I will stand resolute in the face of fear and proclaim the victory of Christ Jesus over my life and circumstances. You have made me strong, and my path is secure in you.

Depth of Love

You have granted me life and steadfast love,
and your care has preserved my spirit.

JOB 10:12 ESV

Thank you, Father, for your favor. I need your presence
close to me today, and I need to know I am loved. Help me
to see how you provide your Spirit to comfort and guide
me in your ways. Thank you that I have life in you because
of what Christ did.

You have not only preserved my spirit, but you have also
blessed me in this life with your mercy and kindness. Help
me to be filled with the knowledge of your will and to
understand the depth of love you have for me.

*God, you keep me secure. Your love is certain and
unending. I do not have to be anything or achieve anything
to deserve your love because your love is unconditional.
You are love, and you exude it in everything you do. You
care about me and want me to prosper in your ways. You
give me life everlasting, and I will trust in you today for my
security.*

Temptations

The temptations in your life are no different from what others experience. And God is faithful. He will not allow the temptation to be more than you can stand. When you are tempted, he will show you a way out so that you can endure.

1 CORINTHIANS 10:13 NLT

God, thank you for your faithfulness. I plead with you to show me a different way quickly, as sin overwhelms me at times. Help me to envision the escape and elude the evil one. I need your strength to sustain me to stand. I want to know your way and welcome your wisdom.

Thank you for promising to provide a path without peril. I pray for your promises to penetrate my perception so I can purposefully walk away from sin. You are the faithful Father who does not fail his followers.

I believe in you, God. You are faithful to me, and you will save me from the fowler's snare. You have provided me a way of escape in each temptation I face. You are a good father, and you give me good advice.

One Sacrifice

With one sacrifice he made perfect forever
those who are being made holy.

HEBREWS 10:14 NCV

Wow, Jesus, that is an amazing feat. Thank you that
despite my failure, I am being made holy. Thank you for
your forgiveness and love. Thank you that though I am not
perfect, you are making me more like you. Help me to be
dependent on your Spirit, like you were when you walked
the earth.

I need you more today than I have ever before. I may not
see it, but I know I do. Jesus, please guide and guard my
heart. Help me to do your will even though everything has
been done to make me right in your eyes.

*God, in one action you made way for the whole world
to be saved. Because of you, Jesus, we are holy. Your
righteousness and devotion to the Father is my covering.
You have set me apart for your purposes, and you will make
a way for me, despite my failings. You are faithful and holy.*

Security of Love

You, God, see the trouble of the afflicted;
you consider their grief and take it in hand.
The victims commit themselves to you;
you are the helper of the fatherless.

PSALM 10:14 NIV

Father, I ask that you would help those who are afflicted as you help me in my suffering. I pray that you would comfort those who have no family and feel alone. Bring them people who will minister to them and help them in their grief.

I pray for the children who have no parents and lack the security of love. Surround them with your presence and fill my heart, and the heart of the Church, to care for them. Help me to do your will in caring for the orphan.

God, you are a kind father, and you care for all who are oppressed and burdened. You love to help those in need and lift the heads of those who are ashamed. I will lift my eyes to look to you in my times of trouble. You are my rock and my fortress. In no person, place, or thing do I have the security that I have in you.

Unbroken Promises

Let us hold firmly to the hope that we have confessed,
because we can trust God to do what he promised.

HEBREWS 10:23 NCV

God, I want to trust in you more. Please help me to be less
reliant on myself, and to let go and let you. I want my heart
to be steadfast in knowing your promises and to patiently
wait upon you.

I pray that through trials and difficulties I would continue
to place my hope in your return and my resurrection to be
with you. I do not want to look to things of this life to give
me endurance, but I want my heart to be set firmly in your
hands.

*God, you are my hope and salvation. I look forward to
experiencing resurrection and living forever with you and
with other believers in our newly created world. You will
do what you have promised. Your Word never returns
void. You are faithful, and I confess that I trust in you. My
confidence comes from your unbroken promises.*

Expectation

The hope of the righteous ends in gladness,
but the expectation of the wicked comes to nothing.

PROVERBS 10:28 NRSV

God, I want to experience joy in knowing you. I ask that the things of this life would grow dim, and that your Spirit would increase in me. I want to be able to devote my heart to seeking you and not be troubled by worldly pursuits.

Help me to be wholehearted in my desire because I know I cannot do this alone. You have to be with me, and mature me, otherwise I am likely to fall short, and like the wicked, come to nothing.

Father, you are my hope and my joy. In you I find fulfillment and peace beyond anything in this life. I will be wholeheartedly engrossed in knowing you and being filled with your Spirit. Because of your faithfulness, I will not fail, but my expectation for resurrection and life in you will come to fruition.

Deep Care

"Don't worry. For your Father cares deeply
about even the smallest detail of your life."

MATTHEW 10:30-31 TPT

Jesus, I love that you said this so confidently. I ask that you would help me to know the Father like you did. I want to feel the security that you felt, so that when trouble comes, and when people speak against me, I will remain steadfast and strong.

I want your assurance to be my delight and your faithfulness to be my joy. I know my propensity to waver in my faith and to pursue the wrong things. Help me to not worry and fear but to be filled with gratitude and faith.

God, you are my delight and nothing else will satisfy. I do not need to worry about my life because you care about it too. You are the best Father I could wish for, and you do take care of me. I am certain that in difficulty and in suffering, you will comfort me and be with me. You are a good father.

Word Recall

"Whoever acknowledges me before others,
I will also acknowledge before my Father in heaven."

MATTHEW 10:32 NIV

Jesus, I struggle with knowing when to speak out and when to let my action be the voice. Help me to listen to your Spirit so that when I face an opportunity to bear witness to you, I will be faithful in doing your will. Also help me to be ready to respond with your Word in season and out of season.

As I read your Word, I ask that it would bear witness in my own heart and that you would help me to remember it, so that I can speak it confidently. I want to recall your Word more frequently, so I ask that you would help my memory and also strengthen my boldness to speak your Word.

You have good news for all men. Your leadership is perfect, and your ways are the right way to live. You have good intentions for your people, and you love those who seek you out. You will equip me to speak your word boldly and to know when to vocalize it and when to act. You are my helper and my guide.

No Favorites

"God does not show favoritism but accepts from every nation the one who fears him and does what is right."

ACTS 10:34–35 NIV

Father, I pray for the nations—that all men would fear you and come to know you. I ask that everywhere people would walk in righteousness and honor for the glory of your name.

I pray in my heart that I would know what it means to fear you while knowing your love and grace. I want to learn what it means to revere you, God, and to honor your name in all that I say and do. Help me to do this today.

You are holy, God. You are righteous and just, and you measure your love and justice equally. You rule and you reign over the heavens and the earth. God you are magnificent in all you do, and your creation is amazing. You are not a God who plays favorites but love those who seek after you, and you reward me when I seek you. You are faithful to do all that you promise, and I trust in you.

Confident Trust

Do not throw away this confident trust in the Lord.
Remember the great reward it brings you!

HEBREWS 10:35 NLT

God, I want to give you my heart fully. Help me to release
my worries and concerns to you and to trust in you. I
usually get anxious because I want to control an outcome
and can't. Help me to leave things in your hands and know
that you want the best for me. I always want to put my
best foot forward and that comes with confidence that
you will back me up. Be close to me so that I can walk with
assurance in knowing your proximity to my every move.

*You are trustworthy, Father. You not only know my needs,
but you have provided everything that sustains me in this
life. I can give my heart to you wholly and know that you
will not fail me. You are a faithful, just, and loving God who
knows what is best for me. I believe in you Jesus: in your
resurrection to eternal life and the great reward you have
for me.*

Mind of Christ

You need to persevere so that when you have done the will of God, you will receive what he has promised.

HEBREWS 10:36 NIV

I struggle to push through temptation and trial. I want your help, Jesus. I tend to want to escape something difficult rather than face it. Help me to be brave in my battles that no one else sees.

Give me the strength that Christ had, the power that enabled him to overcome great suffering and death. This is what I need so I can do your will, God. I want to do your will and I want to receive all that you have for me. I ask for the mind of Christ.

God, you sustain me by your mighty hand. In you I have the endurance to overcome any obstacle and the guidance to go around it when needed. Your power will sustain me through trial and tribulation. You will give me all that I need to have confidence to face even death. It is in you that I find all I need for this life, and I will be confident in your provision.

By Believing

If you openly declare that Jesus is Lord and believe in your heart that God raised him from the dead, you will be saved. For it is by believing in your heart that you are made right with God, and it is by openly declaring your faith that you are saved.

ROMANS 10:9-10 NLT

Jesus, thank you for saving me. I ask that you would help my heart to remain steadfast in you. Develop in me a life devoted to you, that my words and actions would exemplify your love and goodness. Help me to share with others the life that you have given, and the opportunity to be set free from sin and death.

Fill me with your joy and excitement to share the good news with others. I ask that you would be glorified in me as you did for the Father. I also ask that you would help remove from my life those things that do not bring you glory.

You are my Savior. You redeemed me from the enemy and paid for my sin on the cross. You have given me life everlasting through your sacrifice. I believe in you with all my heart, and I give my life back to you for your glory.

Enduring Love

The LORD is good and his love endures forever;
his faithfulness continues through all generations.

PSALM 100:5 NIV

Lord, thank you for your great love. I ask that you would fill me to the brim that I would overflow to others. I want to have such assurance in you that I do not look to anyone, or anything else, for my wellbeing.

I love that you are faithful, and I pray that my trust in you would increase, not because of what I do, but because of who you are, and my knowledge of you. Fill me with your Word, that I may know your promises and be strengthened by your great love.

God, your character is trustworthy. You have been faithful to many generations, and you won't stop with me. I can trust that you will love me forever because you are love. Love does not leave you; it is not persuaded by my performance. Your love is more faithful than the rising of the sun and the going down of the same. I will declare your goodness and your love forever.

Answered

He will answer the prayers of the needy;
he will not reject their prayers.

PSALM 102:17 NCV

Father, help me to know that I can call out to you, and you
will hear me. I need to know that you will answer me too. I
want to let you know my needs and not worry about them.
Help me to be more vulnerable about where I am at in life
and to share with you.

I mentally know you care but I need help with surrendering
my heart and trusting that you have greater intentions for
me than my own. Help me to have success in being like
your Son. I want my heart to pursue the things you want
and not what I want.

*God, you are enough for me. You know my needs before
I even express them. You are faithful to hear and answer
them. You plan good things for me, and my future is
certain. You have given me salvation, your Spirit, and all
that I need to be successful in this life.*

Immeasurable

As high as the heavens are above the earth,
so great is his steadfast love toward those who fear him.

PSALM 103:11 ESV

Lord, I want to grow in understanding the depth of your love for me, and the heights to which you would go to show me it. Open my eyes to the many ways in which you love me and your body. Change my perception to align with the truth of your Word and fill my heart with the same love that you show me, so I can exemplify that love to others.

Help my small human brain to open up and be filled with the knowledge and comprehension of your love. If I don't know it, how will I show it?

God, your love knows no limits. It is not impeded by any of my worst imaginations. Your love overcomes my sin and the depravity of my mind. Your love, demonstrated on the cross, covered over the sins of the world for all generations. It is perfect and immeasurable.

With Compassion

As a father shows compassion to his children,
so the LORD shows compassion to those who fear him.

PSALM 103:13 ESV

God, I want help to show others your compassion. I ask
that you would give me a new ability to look past outward
appearances and see the heart of a person. Help me to
show in action, and through speech, the same sympathy
that you demonstrate to me.

I pray that your grace and mercy for my wrongful actions
would inspire me to mature and not fall further into sin.
Help me be a good son that follows his Father's example.

*I am thankful for your great kindness toward me, God.
You do not condemn me by measuring out what I am
experiencing and weighing that against my weakness and
brokenness. You find me wanting, but you do not leave
me there. You rescue me with mercy and gentleness. Your
compassion and kindness restore me, and I have a clear
path to a great relationship with you.*

Forget Not

Praise the LORD, my soul, and forget not all his benefits—
who forgives all your sins and heals all your diseases.

PSALM 103:2-3 NIV

Father, I am thankful for your forgiveness. In my
brokenness, help me to call out to you and praise you.
When I am angry or upset, I struggle to think about how
great you are. Help me to be mindful of your power,
victory, and control over my life.

Usually in moments of distress, my emotions get the better
of me. Help me to slow down, acknowledge what I am
feeling, and put it in the context of who you are and what
you are doing in my life. Give me your eyes, that I may see
things as you see them. Please heal me of my diseases this
day as you have forgiven me of my sins. Make it real to me
in this life, Jesus.

*God, you have not abandoned me. You are with me
because you are faithful. I praise you because you are
always by my side. Even in my darkest times of trouble or
thought, you are close to me. When I am sick, tired, and
weary, you give me strength to go another day. In you, I
find joy and peace in the worst of circumstances. In you, I
am loved and secure.*

Extravagant Promises

He redeems me from death
and crowns me with love and tender mercies.
He fills my life with good things.
My life is renewed like the eagle's!

PSALM 103:4-5 NLT

Father, why you chose to rescue me sometimes blows my mind. Who am I that you would not only redeem me and pay such a price, but also that you would lavish upon me your daily love and kindness? Help me to see this when I face trouble.

Lift my eyes to see the great things that you have done for me, so I am not overwhelmed with my current circumstances or daily frustrations. Sometimes I feel like I need a jolt to awaken me from my mediocrity and slumber. Stir my heart to the things you have done, are doing, and will do in me.

God, you are my redeemer! You have restored what was lost and in you I have great potential and extravagant promises! What a great God I serve. You are so kind and tender toward me. You are my loving Father, and you lift me up whether good or bad days are upon me.

Compassion and Grace

The LORD is compassionate and gracious,
slow to anger, abounding in love.

PSALM 103:8 NIV

Father, I am in awe of your fervent love for me. I pray that your compassion and grace would surround me today. Open my eyes to how good you are; I need this because I am often caught up in my own anxiety and failings. Give me the same patient peace that you have.

I also ask that as I take in your love and grace, I would grow in my ability to show love to others. Help me to have your patience for them as you do for me. Give me the strength and endurance today to do your will.

God, I will cast all my cares upon you because you care for me. You love me and value me much more than I know. You will show me your love, and you will open my eyes to see your goodness. I trust in you. I give my anxieties to you. I will praise and thank you because of your compassion and grace.

Broken Chains

He brought them out of darkness
and the shadow of death,
and broke their chains in pieces.

PSALM 107:14 NKJV

God, help me to be secure in knowing that you continue to be for me even in my failing. Give me boldness and take away my fear and worry. I want to put my trust in the work you have done for me and the word you promise me.

Garnish me with the strength to face today with newfound passion for you and a sobriety about the works of the enemy. I don't want to be ignorant that he is active in stirring anxiety and dread. I want my heart to be secure and my mind to be sound as I recall your victory over death and the certainty of my future in you.

Mighty King, you have rescued me from the pit, and I love you for it. I no longer am a slave to sin and have no fear of death. You offer me freedom from the grasp of the troubles in this life because in you is security, peace, and victory. I have found the one my heart loves and it is you. You sustain and give me strength to face each day with joy.

Demonstrative Love

He satisfies the longing soul,
and the hungry soul he fills with good things.

PSALM 107:9 ESV

Provider of all my needs, encourage me today to look to you when I long for the wrong things. Fill me with your love and sharpen my mind so that I am not dulled by distractions. Help me to recall your Word and pursue your will as Christ did when he was on earth.

Deepen my understanding of your desire for me and draw me closer to your Spirit. Refresh me, Father, with all that I need today to accomplish what I have set my mind to do. I ask that I would walk according to your will, and that your desires would become mine.

God, you are my satisfaction and delight. I do not need any other. You opened my eyes to you, and I see how great and marvelous you are. You fill my heart with joy and at your right hand are pleasures evermore. Who is there like you? No one knows me like you do! You are excellent and I am astounded by your demonstrative love.

Quiet and Confident

My heart, O God, is quiet and confident,
all because of you.
Now I can sing my song with passionate praises!
Awake, O my soul, with the music of his splendor.

PSALM 108:1 TPT

I need your help, God, to pray this into existence. I want my heart to be quiet and confident. I want to be able to see all that is happening in life and not be anxious or overwhelmed. I ask for increased faith to fill my heart and mind, so I can envision the things you are doing and praise you for them.

Place in me your promises; plant them in the soil of my heart, so when I go into the world and encounter temptation and trial, I will be so full of your Word that I won't succumb to the enemy. Fill me with your wonder and thoughts of your greatness.

Father, I know when my heart is troubled, you can give me songs and awaken me to you. You are trustworthy and care for me. I find in you the peace and security that I need. You seal my heart with your promises, and in them I have eternal hope and assurance of things to come. You are faithful to fulfill your Word.

Increased Faith

Faith is confidence in what we hope for
and assurance about what we do not see.

HEBREWS 11:1 NIV

Jesus, help me, as you have helped so many, to have increased faith. Fulfill in me the promises that you made to generations of saints who are now with you. Be my guide today in everything I do and lead me by your strong hand.

I need to know the same confidence that you had in your Father each day. I want to grow in my ability to let go of the things of this life and take hold of your promises for my future in you. Give me your eyes to see, Jesus.

You made a way for me to know you, Jesus. Because of you I have eternal life and an inheritance that will never fade or perish. I do not fear entrapment and death because you have set me free. I no longer am controlled by sin but am filled with your Spirit who enables me to accomplish your will. You are good to me!

Synced

"I tell you, whatever you ask in prayer,
believe that you have received it,
and it will be yours."

MARK 11:24 ESV

Jesus, I want to be filled with greater faith. Help me in my unbelief! There are many things I want to ask for, but I know that some of them are my desires and not yours. Help me to be in sync with your Spirit so that I request the right things and can therefore be assured of the outcome.

I want to walk in a manner that exemplifies Christ, so give me the daily strength to trust in your same desire for me. You and I want the same thing in my spiritual life, so I pray that this would be fulfilled in me. Fill me with your Spirit!

Jesus, you are faithful in listening to me and answering me. You are seated at the right hand of God the Father, praying for me. You want more for me than I can understand, so I will trust in you. I will join you in prayer, assured that you will answer.

Infused Life

"I am the resurrection and the life.
The one who believes in me will live,
even though they die;
and whoever lives by believing in me will never die."

JOHN 11:25-26 NIV

Jesus, I want to live my life like death is not something I have to worry about. Help me to believe your words, and to not worry about the things of this world. I get overwhelmed by responsibilities and decisions sometimes, and I want help to put them in the perspective of eternity.

I want more of your life to be infused into mine. I want the power of your Spirit, that resurrected you from the dead, to fill me afresh today.

Jesus, you made the way for me to live for eternity. You are the way, the truth, and the life. In you, I have assurance that my sacrifices in this life will result in rewards in eternity. I know that you have provided everything I need right now and have even more for me in the future. Thank you!

Finding Rest

"Come to me,
all you who are weary and burdened,
and I will give you rest."

MATTHEW 11:28 NIV

Jesus, I want to come to you first. I know my heart goes to other things to find rest, and they do not give me what I need. I look to be entertained or numbed by many distractions, and I miss out on what you have for me.

Turn my eyes to you, Jesus. May my heart be persuaded to pursue you first before any other opportunity for relief. Help me to do the hard work of seeking you out when I am weary and burdened.

You are sweet relief, Jesus. I will find the peace, relaxation, and joy that I need when I come to you. My hope will not be disappointed. My experience of you will produce the rest that I need, and my life will be enriched by your presence. I will be a better man because I came to you.

Gentle King

"Take my yoke upon you and learn from me,
for I am gentle and humble in heart,
and you will find rest for your souls."

MATTHEW 11:29 NIV

Jesus, for some reason it seems easier to run to the things of this world for rest. Perhaps it is because I live in the world, but what I really want is for my heart to turn to you first. I know you can use the things of this life to bless and rest me. So, I ask that you would help me to set you before me always, so my mind and heart would immediately turn to you when I face trouble.

You want me to engage you and grow in you, but I need your help to do that. I want to know the ease of living learning from you.

You are faithful to do your will in me. Jesus, I trust that you have the best in mind for me, so I give you my heart, and I will devote my mind to seeking the things of you. You are a gentle servant-king to those who love you.

MARCH

We are confident that
he hears us whenever
we ask for anything
that pleases him.

1 JOHN 5:14 NLT

See the Unseen

It is by faith we understand that the whole world was made by God's command so what we see was made by something that cannot be seen.

HEBREWS 11:3 NCV

God, I want to have my eyes opened to see what you see. It must be glorious and terrifying all at once. I want to be more aware of what is happening in the heavens as much as I am able to see around me on earth. I ask that it would cause me to be sober: that I would pray more, that I would fight for justice, and that I would love sacrificially.

Help me to understand what you are doing in this time, so my life and responses would align with your kingdom and your plans.

Father, you are so powerful and wonderful. When I dwell upon how the world was formed by your word, I am amazed at your magnanimous heart and magnificent creativity. You gave so much to create something you knew would cause you pain, and still you did it. You have a generous heart!

Increase Faith

Without faith living within us it would be impossible to please God. For we come to God in faith knowing that he is real and that he rewards the faith of those who give all their passion and strength into seeking him.

HEBREWS 11:6 TPT

Father, thank you that I can please you at all. I have faith in you, but it is weak, so I ask that you would increase my faith. I pray that I would remain strong knowing you are the God of the impossible and you do not relent in pursuing those who turn to you.

Help me to be fervent in my desire for you and to always look to you in my good times and bad times. I want my faith to be strong in times of testing. Enable me to remember your promises in the midst of adversity.

God, you reward those who love you and seek you. You reward me with life everlasting and you strengthen me to endure. Thank you for your goodness. You are active in my life today. You are living and active!

No Offense

"Blessed is anyone who
takes no offense at me."

MATTHEW 11:6 NRSV

Jesus, if I become hard of heart and stop pursuing you, please break into my soul and turn me around. I don't ever want to become separated from you, so I ask that you would continue to soften my heart toward you and keep me as you promised to keep me.

I ask that you would help me to not be offensive to you. I know you hate pride and will not accept the prideful in your kingdom. Keep my heart secure in you so I do not become self-reliant and guarded. Keep me open and protect my heart.

God, you will never leave me or forsake me. You do not abandon those who love and pursue you. You will never turn away a son who returns to you. You are faithful and ever loving. There is nothing that I can do to make your heart hard. Thank you for your everlasting love.

Just and Good

All he does is just and good,
and all his commandments are trustworthy.

PSALM 111:7 NLT

Father, I may not always understand your ways, but I ask you to help me believe in your character. I want to understand you on a deeper level; open my heart so I comprehend you in a new way.

Let my eyes not be darkened by the world and its distractions; give me your Spirit so I can encounter you intimately. You have so much more for me that I miss out on because I give my mind to other things. Help me to realign myself with you.

I am sure of your goodness and your right judgments. You are trustworthy and your Word is true. Your leadership is perfect, and I can trust in your commands and the actions you take. I know no other as great as you, God, and I am thankful for your love and kindness toward me.

Walking Honestly

A light shines in the dark for honest people,
for those who are merciful and kind and good.

PSALM 112:4 NCV

Father, I want to be led by you in my darkest hour. It is hard for me to be merciful, kind, and good when I am in need and when I am struggling. I usually want others to help me, or to stay away so I can figure things out. My heart is not always in the best place, but I need your light to shine all the time!

Help me to see you in all circumstances and to walk honestly before you. I want to be a person who demonstrates the grace and kindness to others that you show to me.

God, you are a bright and true light, leading all who look to you with clarity and honesty. Your leadership is perfect. I love that you care about those who live with integrity and that you want to reward us in this life as well as with an eternal inheritance. You are a faithful father, and I can depend on you.

Return to Rest

Return to your rest, my soul,
for the LORD has been good to you.

PSALM 116:7 NIV

Lord, help me to rest in you. I want to know what it means to lay in green pastures by still waters. I want to know how to live without wanting because I have what I need. Help me to want what I have so I am satisfied in you.

Remind me of your assurances throughout the day and help me to place my hope in you and your Word. I desire that my striving would cease and that I would know peace today. Grant me the vision to see your goodness and the fortitude to remain faithful.

God, you provide the sustenance and goodness I need so I can relax. I can trust in your ways and your promises. You have good things in store for me. Even in my trials and difficulties you stand with me and give me what I need to be strong. I have more than enough to live a satisfied life because of you.

Enduring Truth

His merciful kindness is great toward us,
And the truth of the Lord endures forever.
Praise the Lord!

PSALM 117:2 NKJV

Father, would you fill me with your truth, so I am overflowing to others? Holy Spirit come upon me today so I can give to others what you have given to me. I ask that your Word would help me to understand my place in you and break off any deception that would say otherwise.

I know when I am secure in you, I can love others better, so I pray that you would give me this revelation today.

God, I love that you are merciful toward me! Thank you for being a great father who loves so well. I am overjoyed that you have chosen me as your child and that you continue to give me all I need to grow up in your home. I am being made into the person you desire—a mature man in Christ. I believe in your Word and that you fill me with your truth by the work of your Holy Spirit.

What Is Better

It is better to take refuge in the Lord
than to trust in people.

PSALM 118:8 NLT

God, my heart looks easily to man. When I look to others, I find that my heart is swayed in many directions. I want you to help me to attune my thoughts to you when I am in need.

I ask that you would give me awareness of when I am seeking out people and it is leading me in a wrong direction. When you show me this, give me strength to choose you and turn my affections, attentions, and desires over to you. Help me to trust you, Father.

You are faithful. You won't let me down, God. I can be confident in your Word. What you say will take place. I have no reason to doubt you except for my own broken experiences. You are my healer! You take what is dirty, broken, and valueless, and restore it. You are awesome. Thank you.

Source of Hope

You are my refuge and my shield;
your word is my source of hope.

PSALM 119:114 NLT

Why is my heart so fickle, God? I seem to be easily taken
by what the world offers me. I'm so quickly kidnapped
by the arousal of other affections. Help me to be more
resolute in coming to you. Show me the things you have
given me and help me to want them above the passions of
this life.

Give me your self-control and Spirit of truth. Fill me with
your Word and help me recall it when I need it most. Thank
you for your promise to get me out of trouble at all times.

*God, you are my only hope. You are the reason I fight to
do what is right. I know you have promises beyond this
life that are so much better than what I have now or what
tempts me. You created all good things, and the pleasure
I experience in this life will be magnified greatly in your
presence. You are completely satisfying!*

Proximity

You are near, O Lord,
and all your commands are true.

PSALM 119:151 NLT

Father, I want to know your proximity to my process. I want to know that you are close when I am making my choices. I ask for your Word to be welcome in my mind. Help my heart to commandeer your commands and follow them.

I ask for your faithfulness to be at the forefront of my mind when I flail in my misfortune. Grant me the wisdom to avoid paths that wander away from you. Guide my steps, God.

Thank you for how close you are to me, God. You walk with me when I am strong, you let me lean on you when I am weak, and you carry me when I fall. You are a faithful friend who is a strong fortress in times of trouble. I can come to you with all my burdens, and you make them light. Thank you for the truth of your Word and how it helps me to walk a straight path.

Essence of Truth

The very essence of your words is truth;
all your just regulations will stand forever.

PSALM 119:160 NLT

God, I tell myself I need your words to fill my heart and
mind. I want to think your thoughts. I ask that you would
help me to retain your Word in my mind so I can stand
forever with you.

I want to be filled with a hunger for justice. Even though
my perspective is limited, help me to do right by those
around me. Help me to be filled with love, truth, and justice,
so the world sees you in me.

*What you speak and how you live are true and just, God.
You are love, and out of you come the right words in the
right season. I trust what you say and believe in its veracity.
Your voice is the only one I need to hear. Your words bring
life to me. I trust in your justice and your law, and I honor
your name by following after you.*

No Stumbling

Those who love your instructions
have great peace and do not stumble.

PSALM 119:165 NLT

Father, it is difficult to follow you and not choose my own way. Give me the same passion and knowledge that Jesus had when he walked the earth. Fill me with your Spirit so I can experience you with me in everything I go through.

Jesus, you knew the Father and pursued him so well. I want to know you, God, in the same way. I know that even though Jesus went through difficulties, he had peace and did not falter because of his trust in you. Give me this same trust Jesus.

You are worthy of my adoration, God. You are trustworthy and true. All of your promises will come to pass. I know your salvation now, and I will experience your resurrection. You are my rock and my redeemer, and I will continue to trust in you. Fill my heart with your Spirit and keep me. You will never leave me nor forsake me.

Comfort in Suffering

My comfort in my suffering is this:
your promise preserves my life.

PSALM 119:50 NIV

Jesus, you understand this prayer more than anyone. Help me to trust in the Father's words like you trusted. You knew that he would not forsake you and I ask that you would help me in the same way: to know that I will never be left especially as I am troubled.

Help my heart to always be led back to you, God. I don't want distractions and other worries to overwhelm me when I am need. I want your Spirit to overshadow me and help me in my times of need and my times of joy.

You are my greatest comfort, Father. You provide me your Spirit to bring peace to my soul and to help me recollect your marvelous deeds. You show me your Word and make it a light to my path. You are the one who I need more than any other. It is in you, Jesus, that I find everything for life and godliness.

Benefits and Rewards

Wise words bring many benefits,
and hard work brings rewards.

PROVERBS 12:14 NLT

Father, help me to listen to wisdom and not turn away from the good things that you provide for me each day. I want to know your Word and put it into action. And I want those actions to bring glory to you.

Help me to work hard not just for my own gain, but for your kingdom. Help me to see beyond this life and consider my future in you and my reward at the end of the age. Give me an eternal perspective on my life today.

You are God eternal. You have all of the world in mind, and you know me intimately. How amazing you are God! You reward those who diligently seek you and you are faithful to do what you say you will. I will put my trust in the wisdom of your words, and I will diligently work hard to further your kingdom above my own. You are master of the universe!

Trusted Leadership

If the whole body were an eye, it would not be able to hear. If the whole body were an ear, it would not be able to smell. If each part of the body were the same part, there would be no body. But truly God put all the parts, each one of them, in the body as he wanted them.

1 CORINTHIANS 12:17-18 NCV

Jesus, thank you for the people who are part of your body. Help me to love those who are not the same as me. Help me to see the value of each person I meet and love them as you love them.

I ask that you would help all of us to look to one another for help, and to be strengthened by the gifts that you have placed in each of us. Immerse us in your Spirit and bring unity to us.

Thank you that you have given me a part in your body, Father. Thank you that you have made me unique and that you have plans for my life far beyond what I can see. You are a masterful builder, and you know how to intricately engage each of us in your plans. I trust in your leadership, Jesus.

Joy in Difficulty

Looking to Jesus the pioneer and perfecter of our faith, who for the sake of the joy that was set before him endured the cross, disregarding its shame, and has taken his seat at the right hand of the throne of God.

HEBREWS 12:2 NRSV

Father, help me to look to Jesus. I find myself caught up in the worries of this life too often. There is so much to do and not enough time. Help me to set aside moments with you—just you. Give me your focus and strength so I can be like Jesus, trusting in you and listening to your Spirit.

I want to know you more and be filled with the same joy that Jesus had even when facing difficulty.

You are my helper, God. I am thankful that you give me the strength to face each day and do the things that you want me to do. You are strong, and I do not have to worry about being overcome. You watch over me and help me in my toughest moments. Thank you, Jesus.

From Deep Within

Behold, God is my salvation,
I will trust and not be afraid;
For the LORD God is my strength and my song,
And He has become my salvation.

ISAIAH 12:2 NASB

Father, when my heart is fearful and overwhelmed by my circumstances, please give me your perspective. Embolden my soul to step out and trust you. Be my sustenance and joy in the midst of the hardest times and my satisfaction when I am cruising.

Help me to sing to you from deep within my heart and not hold back. I want my soul to look to you at all times, so I am not afraid of anything I face.

God, you are my rock and shield. You stand before my enemies and laugh at their weak ways. You have no nemesis to plan for, no power you fear, no worry that overcomes you. You are Yahweh, Almighty God, Everlasting Father, and faithful friend. I have no concern that you are not aware of or that you cannot subdue. I can trust in you!

For Him

The Lord will not abandon His people on account of His great name, because the Lord has been pleased to make you a people for Himself.

1 Samuel 12:22 nasb

Jesus, thank you that you have chosen all of your people. I am one of those and I ask that you would help me to live like a son who has a king for a dad. I want to have confidence in everything I do because you back me up.

Help me to make the right choices and to live in a way that pleases you. What I don't want is to find myself running off doing things that don't matter to you and planning things outside your will. Give me your eyes and your heart, so I can live for you.

God, you are good. You do the right things. You are the way, the truth, and the life. You hold me in your hands. I choose to do the things that please you because you have given me everything I need to do so. I believe in your faithful words and ways, and I know that your assurances are good. Your guarantee for life is eternal.

Fixed

Since we are receiving a kingdom that cannot be shaken, let us be thankful, and so worship God acceptably with reverence and awe.

HEBREWS 12:28 NIV

God, fill my heart with gratitude and admiration for you. Please help me to be more grateful and delight in who you are. When I am overcome by this world, give me your perspective, and fill me with worship.

My heart is easily dissuaded when things don't work out the way I want. Let me be fixed on you and your promises. Refocus my life so it aligns with the things you are thinking and doing.

You are uncompromising when it comes to your Word and the love that you have for me, Father God. I have no need to worry or be afraid because you are so strong and faithful. I will not allow the anxiety of this life to prevent me from expressing my worship and praise to you. Nor will life make me unhappy because I will practice thankfulness in all that I do.

Drink Deeply

With joy you will drink deeply
from the fountain of salvation.

PSALM 12:3 NLT

Father, I don't know what I can do to know more of you except to read your Word and ask you to fill me with your Spirit. I want to be better at seeking you out in all that I do.

Find ways for my heart to be drawn to you and help me to seek your pleasure before my own. I want to know what it means to be filled with your joy every day.

God, you have living water that will satisfy me forever. Thank you for providing joy and pleasure that will never go away. Thank you for your Holy Spirit who dwells with me every day to satisfy the longing of my heart. You are my salvation and my eternal reward. My heart delights in you always, and my hope is set upon my resurrection in you and the inheritance of eternal delight.

Every Need

"People everywhere seem to worry about making a living, but your heavenly Father knows your every need and will take care of you."

LUKE 12:30 TPT

People everywhere includes me. Father, I have to confess that I am overwhelmed with things to do because I want to take care of myself. I tend to add more to my life than less, which makes me worry about things even though I shouldn't.

Help me to leave myself in your hands and lay down my independence. I want to learn to depend on you more without it costing me too much. But I think you want me to lay down everything, so you can give me what you want. Help me to trust you to do this.

God, you are my provider and my boss. You know what jobs I need and what things I should be doing: things that both help me to grow and things that you want me to do for your kingdom. I trust in you and rest in knowing that you are faithful and that you continue to look out for me each day.

Different Ways

God works in different ways,
but it is the same God who does the work in all of us.

1 CORINTHIANS 12:6 NLT

Father, I have noticed that you do things differently with each of us. Give me your wisdom so I can treat others as they need to be treated. Help me to see with your eyes and not to judge too quickly.

Help me when I get frustrated that others are not changing; it is me that you want to change. Help me to be patient too, knowing that you are working in each of us to help us be mature in you.

You are an inspiration, God. You do things so well and you know us all intimately. You are thoughtful and caring and actively involved in our lives. You have good intentions for me, and I know that you will keep your word, which is good and right. You have plans for my life that will benefit my soul.

Empowered

He said to me, "My grace is sufficient for you, for my power is made perfect in weakness." Therefore I will boast all the more gladly about my weaknesses, so that Christ's power may rest on me.

2 Corinthians 12:9 niv

Jesus, sometimes I hate my weakness and I don't want to rely on others. It is my independence that gets me in trouble so much. Give me your ability to trust the Father and lean on other believers. Help me to embrace my lesser skills and utilize others' strengths to overcome.

Show me where I am depending on myself and not looking to you. It is better for me to be weak and empowered by you than to be strong and run out of my own power, which I do regularly.

Father, you are for me, and you will give me what I need to be empowered throughout today. I can trust in you to make me brave, strong, productive, loving, and kind. I know these qualities do not come to me naturally, but you have them all. Thank you for sharing them with me.

Selfless Joy

Be joyful.
Grow to maturity.
Encourage each other.
Live in harmony and peace.
Then the God of love and peace will be with you.

2 CORINTHIANS 13:11 NLT

Lord, help me to be a better man for other people. I know that I love myself and look to take care of myself first. However, you ask me to love and think of others first. You want me to be a peacemaker, a lover, and a person of justice.

I want to take joy in these things and to do them with a fervent heart. Help me to serve others and to demonstrate a maturity that encourages unity among others.

Father, you are a God of selfless joy. You are love, and everything you do is from a heart of love. There is not evil intention in you. I know that I can trust you explicitly and that your Word will come to pass. I love your faithfulness and your desire to be with your people—to be with me. I am excited to be a part of your kingdom and to live in the presence of your love forevermore.

Last Forever

Three things will last forever—
faith, hope, and love—
and the greatest of these is love.

1 CORINTHIANS 13:13 NLT

Father, it is great to think of how we will live together forever. Nothing else will remain but relationships and qualities like these: faith, hope, and love. Keep my heart pursuing your love. Build my faith. Help my hope in you to flourish and flow over to others.

Most of all, I want to learn how to love people in a way that demonstrates you to them. I want others to feel like they were cherished and cared for, and that I had good intentions in all that I did with them. Just like you do with me.

You are so good, Jesus. I know that your love is outstanding. There is no comparison for the love that you have toward all mankind. It makes me feel so good knowing that same love is directed toward me. You do not hold back or keep me from you. You are for me and not against me. Thank you.

Faithful Tutor

Spend time with the wise and you will become wise.
but the friends of fools will suffer.

PROVERBS 13:20 NCV

Father, thank you for the people you have put around me
who are wise and understanding. Help me to turn to those
you have given for advice and counsel. I pray that I would
never be too proud to seek out knowledge from others.

Help my heart to be open but also discerning, so I can
know what path to take and when to cast aside man's
opinions. Help my heart to be attuned to your words and
your ways, God.

*You are wise and intelligent, God. You have the knowledge
that I seek, and you care about me. I love that I can come
to you, and you do not despise my simplicity. Anyone who
seeks understanding from you is given it. You give wisdom
in abundance and do so willingly. Who else can help me like
you? No one. You are my faithful tutor in all things of life.*

Righteous Reward

Trouble pursues the sinner,
but the righteous are rewarded with good things.

PROVERBS 13:21 NIV

Lord, I don't want my sins catching up to me. I want to be far from them. Forgive me again for the things I do wrong and change my heart to seek after what is right. You have to help me because I am weak and have a propensity to chase after the desirous things of this world.

You, on the other hand, teach me and show me how to live, and I want to follow you. Give me strength and strategy to walk in your ways and not be found wanting when you return.

You are coming back, Jesus. You have promised that you will return and that when you do you will separate the tares from the wheat and the wolves from the sheep. The sinner will be banished from your presence and the righteous rewarded. You are just and right in doing this and you do it out of mercy and love for those who seek after you. You are a faithful warrior king and priest.

Satisfied

Don't love money; be satisfied with what you have.
For God has said, "I will never fail you.
I will never abandon you."

HEBREWS 13:5 NLT

Father, I want to know in my heart that I do not need any
other. I just want to know the peace of having your love
in my heart and develop dependence upon you. Show me
how I can do this to a greater measure, so there is no other
love or passion in my life that replaces you.

I want to wholeheartedly seek you, and you know how
wayward I am. I need you to be my life and light and to take
my heart and make it yours completely, so I am ready for
your return. I know that is what you want, and I want it too.

*Thank you for your kindness and mercy, Jesus. It leads
me to repentance. You will come back, and I will be ready
because you promise to sustain me. I can rest in knowing
that you will get me there. You will satisfy me.*

The Same

Jesus Christ is the same
yesterday, today, and forever.

HEBREWS 13:8 NKJV

Jesus, I love this. I need this. I have to have something in my life that is not going to crumble and change. I need constant security even though I never would let anyone know that. Help me to stop relying on myself and to embrace dependence on you. I know you can do this in me.

I ask, Holy Spirit, that you would not pass me by, but, as you did with Jesus, place in my heart a God beacon that stops me being disoriented by anything the world offers. Let it shine brightly, so I stay focused on him alone.

Holy Spirit, you dwell in my heart and orient me toward God. Thank you for filling me with a consistent presence of God's love and kindness. You bring comfort to my heart and teach me God's ways. You help me to stay focused and give me what I need each day to follow Jesus.

Drifting

The Lord will work out his plans for my life—
for your faithful love, O Lord, endures forever.
Don't abandon me, for you made me.

PSALM 138:8 NLT

Father, I find my heart drifting often. I know that you have compassion for me and bring me back around. But I get so easily persuaded by other things. Somehow, I need you to protect my heart and secure me in your hand.

I ask for help in trusting you and allowing myself time to sit and wait upon you. I don't want to jump ahead of what you are doing. Give me patience to stand still until you lead me.

You are not overwhelmed by my circumstances, God. You have a plan for me that is far beyond what I can see at the moment. I will trust in the goodness of your heart and the truth that you love me beyond what I can ever know. How wonderful are your ways and the plans that you have for me! I will trust in you, Father.

Even Greater

"I tell you the truth, anyone who believes in me will do the same works I have done, and even greater works, because I am going to be with the Father."

JOHN 14:12 NLT

Holy Spirit, fill me with the power of God to do the things you want me to do. Give me a devoted heart that is full of your love, a mind that has your thoughts, and a will that follows your ways. When this happens, I am confident that I, with others who are in the same place, will see greater things done in your name.

Oh, God, help us to get there: to the place where we are so sold out to you that there are marvelous God sightings all over the planet. I know you want this more than I do, so I ask you to make it happen in us. Purify your bride.

You are a mighty God. You want to demonstrate your power and awe. But you are also kind and loving. Your patience and mercy are evident in every day that humanity continues. A day will come when you return, and your power and authority will be on display. Prepare your bride!

APRIL

You will call on me and
come and pray to me,
and I will listen to you.

JEREMIAH 29:12 NIV

Whatever You Ask

"Whatever you ask in my name, this I will do,
that the Father may be glorified in the Son."

JOHN 14:13 ESV

Jesus, thank you for your words that encourage my faith. I know that you want the Father glorified in all that I do, and I ask that you would help me to honor your desire. I want to be a son, like you, who pleases the Father and asks for the things that are on his heart not my own.

Help me to be filled with your desires and to focus on what matters most to you. I know there is more for me to learn, so please show me how I can grow in you.

You are faithful to me, Jesus. You will work in me the things that you want to do, and I trust that my own plans will not hinder your mighty Spirit. You are going to be glorified in my life, and I give my day to you so you will have your way in me. I surrender to you.

Fight for You

"The Lord will fight for you,
you have only to be still."

Exodus 14:14 NIV

Wow, I need this right now. Sometimes I want to fight all my battles with words and actions that are not Christlike at all. Help me, Jesus, to submit my heart to you first. I need your guidance and Spirit to carry me. Fight for me please and show yourself for the great God that you are.

I surrender my will to you and pray you would give me the strength to wait upon you and not take my own actions. Help me to pray and to fight the right battle and not focus on flesh and blood but to be aware of the spirit realm.

You are Lord of all. You have authority over all things and your power is unending. I can throw myself on your mercy and you carry me. You fight for me, Jesus. I can trust in you. Thank you for sustaining me in my weakest moments.

Not an Orphan

"No, I will not abandon you as orphans—
I will come to you."

JOHN 14:18 NLT

Sometimes, I need to settle down and trust that you will take care of me. My independence and self-service lead me to be an orphan heart of my own accord. Help me to come back to you early and often, Jesus. Fill me with a sense of my great need, the one you see, and help me to turn to you in it.

I am nothing without your mercy each day, and I know when I do not face you and see myself in your reflection, I lose my sense of identity and purpose. Help me to turn my eyes to you.

Jesus, you will not leave or forsake me! Thank you for giving yourself to me and for constantly loving me. You are faithful even when I am not. I can trust in your goodness and your plans for my future. You have assured me that you will come and get me one day. I do not need to worry about my future because it is in your hands.

Many Rooms

> "There are many rooms in my Father's house;
> I would not tell you this if it were not true.
> I am going there to prepare a place for you."
>
> JOHN 14:2 NCV

You are awesome, Jesus. I am excited by what you are preparing for me. You have something for me to do and a place for me to live in your new creation. Now I just need your help to get there!

Give me the strength and vision to hold onto this hope. Help me to continue to trust in your words and to devote my heart to your plans. I want what I do on this earth to prepare me for your kingdom to come and to make way for your return.

You will return to restore your creation and make new the earth, Creator God. I will dwell with you in this place with my brothers and sisters, and we will live, laugh, and love together forever. You are faithful to do all that you promise, and I can have assurance that in you I will be resurrected to life eternal.

The Advocate

"The Advocate, the Holy Spirit, whom the Father will send in my name, will teach you all things and will remind you of everything I have said to you."

JOHN 14:26 NIV

Holy Spirit, fill me with your love. Help me to know your presence like Jesus did when he walked with you. I know that in you, I can remember his Word, and follow his ways, so I ask for your strength and enabling.

Continue to teach me each day so I can represent you well on earth. Give me your perspective so I endure all things as Jesus did. Remind me of your empowering joy, and your gracious love.

Father, thank you for your Spirit sent to teach, counsel, and guide me. Holy Spirit, I love that you are with me now. I find joy in your presence, and I learn more each day about the Father because of you. You give me the words to speak and the thoughts of God to dwell upon.

Well Done

Those who fear the LORD are secure;
he will be a refuge for their children.

PROVERBS 14:26 NLT

God, help me to know what it means to revere your name.
I don't want a fiery bush to appear suddenly, but I do
want your Spirit to be evident in my life and in what I do.
Give me security in a world that is full of change so I may
endure until the end.

In my floundering, fill me with your fire. In my failing, lavish
your love upon me. Gently, yet sternly, guide my heart back
to you at all times. I want to hear those words, "Well done,
good and faithful servant."

*You are my refuge, God. In no other name is their salvation
and resurrection to everlasting life. How can I place
my hope in any other thing? You have given me every
opportunity and equipped me to be successful in you! By
your Word and your Spirit, I have refuge in you forever!*

Perfect Peace

"Peace I leave with you; my peace I give you.
I do not give to you as the world gives.
Do not let your hearts be troubled
and do not be afraid."

JOHN 14:27 NIV

Father, you have given me your peace for the good of my soul. Help me to rest in it. Fill my heart with tranquility so I can love others fully. My peace is lost when I look to the world and forget your promises. Remind me of your Word when I am overwhelmed; bring to mind your promises so I remain faithful to you.

Help me not to look to man as my hope, but to find joy in suffering as Jesus did, anticipating his return and your restoration of all things.

Jesus, you are the man of perfect peace. I resign myself to trusting in your Word and your promises because in you alone is my hope and future. Continue to pour out joy and peace over my life. I know this comes from your Spirit alone.

Fountain of Life

The fear of the LORD is a fountain of life,
turning a person from the snares of death.

PROVERBS 14:27 NIV

Taking in your precepts and your wisdom is a guard for
me, Jesus. Show me your ways and let not my heart
be troubled with the things of this world. You know my
thoughts and what I need. Give me your heart and your
eyes and let temptation and distress fall by the wayside.

I want my heart to be consumed with the things of you.
Make me a temple that is pleasing for your Spirit to dwell
in. It is you, Holy Spirit, that fills me to overflowing, so
please make me a fountain that pours out for others.

*Holy Spirit, you are my truth and light in a dark world. Teach
me the ways of Christ, as I take in his words. You are my
source for joy and comfort. I will turn to you in dark times.
You strengthen me to endure, to last until Jesus returns!*

Preparing a Place

"If I go and prepare a place for you,
I will come back and take you to be with me
that you also may be where I am."

JOHN 14:3 NIV

Father, it is humbling enough that Jesus was sent to redeem me when my sin is what separated us. Now, even more humbling is your kindness in preparing a place for me. I want to endure all that you have for me, so I please you in return.

I want to be ready. Help me to prepare the bride for your Son. Give me your words so I can share you with others and allow them to see your mercy and kindness.

For so great a King, how kind of you to love me. You have chosen to see me, a blip compared to all of life, and yet you pour out your mercy on me. You are for me, and you have a place set aside in lieu of my enduring faithfulness, which is completed only because of who you are in me. Thank you, Jesus.

Peaceful Words

God is not a God of confusion
but a God of peace.

1 CORINTHIANS 14:33 NCV

God, how many times have I been overwhelmed by my
thoughts and you rescued me? I need you more than I
know, and I am reminded by verses like this of how true
and peaceful your words of life are. Give me more of your
clarity and simplicity.

Help me to focus my attention on loving you first and
loving others as an outcome. Pour out your Spirit on me so
I can pour into others your meaningful words of joy. Speak
through me to others your life and peace. May your Spirit
be evident within me.

*Father, you are the God of truth and love. Your mercy is
evident in how patient you are with me. Continue to pour
out your Spirit upon me that I may bless others. You are
absolutely perfect in the way you do things. I do not doubt
your ways and I trust in your leadership.*

One Way

"I am the way, the truth, and the life.
No one can come to the Father except through me."

JOHN 14:6 NLT

Jesus, you made a way for me to be right with the Father
and I am thankful. Help me to turn my heart to you and
to trust in your way of doing things. Often, I struggle to
wait upon you and want to do things without pausing and
listening for your voice.

Show me how you did it when you walked the earth, so I
can do it in preparation for you walking the earth again.
Also, I ask that you would help me to share your way, your
truth, and your life with those around me.

*Jesus, your ways are perfect. There is no other path to know
God except through accepting the salvation you provided.
Thank you for your salvation and your truth that shows me
the way to live. It is because of you that I am saved.*

Steadfast Hope

The Lord is righteous in everything he does;
he is filled with kindness.
The Lord is near to all who call on him,
yes, to all who call on him in truth.

Psalm 145:17-18 nlt

Lord God, I need you close to me. I cry out for your comfort and your Word to draw near to me. Help my heart to be drawn to your kindness, so I am not led astray by the worries of life.

Fill me with your truth and your promises that I would stand firm in good times or bad. You can help me remain faithful even when I am at my weakest. I ask for you to be my steadfast hope.

When I call upon you, God, you answer me. Thank you for being so attentive to my cry. I love your mercies that are new every morning and the joy I find when I give myself to pursuing you. You have made me righteous by the sacrifice of your Son, and this allows me to draw close to you every day. You are always nearby.

Laced with Love

The LORD is gracious and compassionate,
slow to anger and rich in love.
The LORD is good to all;
he has compassion on all he has made.

PSALM 145:8-9 NIV

Father, my compassion and anger-control are lacking. Help me to be like you more often. I know I need to relinquish my desire to regulate everything and make sure it goes my way. I need to be able to trust you as Christ did when he walked the earth.

Strengthen my will to obey you and believe in your love and compassion toward me. Give me the ability to love others in a manner that makes them feel valued and cared for.

God, I trust in you because you do all things right and you are faithful to do what you say. Your judgments are laced with love and carry compassion. You are good to me at all times, and you are gentle in how you deal with me. Thank you for your mercies which are new every morning.

Fully Restored

You open the eyes of the blind
and you fully restore those bent over with shame.
You love those who love and honor you.

PSALM 146:8 TPT

I know that you love to lift up the downhearted. Help me to reach out to those who have need: to be like you by encouraging and strengthening them. Show me your heart toward others so I am not so self-absorbed and unaware of those around me.

Use me to open the eyes of the blind and to cover the shame of the downtrodden. You have the love and compassion that I desire, and I pray for it to be poured out in me for those who are suffering.

God, you give me love and joy to share with others. You have lifted my head so many times when I have been covered with shame. Your enduring love gives me hope and aids in my ability to live each day. You consider those who need, who are humble, who are broken, and you love them well. You have the power to heal and the knowledge that gives understanding. Thank you for sharing your Spirit with me so I can do what Jesus did for others.

My Delight

The LORD delights in those who fear him,
who put their hope in his unfailing love.

PSALM 147:11 NIV

Lord, you are my delight. Help me to revere you and
to understand your holiness. Show me your power and
authority over all things so I may stand in awe of your
majestic ways. Open my eyes to your creation and the
beauty of what you have made around me.

I want to be able to recognize your handiwork and the
creativity with which you made all things. I pray that my
heart would be as faithful as your unfailing love and that
my hope would remain strong as I longingly wait for your
return.

*You are coming back, Jesus. You will fulfill your Word,
destroying evil, and restoring creation. I will wait patiently
for you to return. I will endure, and I will make it because
of your faithfulness and endless love. I am full of hope
because I know I can trust in you. How great are your ways,
O God!*

My Provider

Give generously to them and do so without a grudging heart; then because of this the Lord your God will bless you in all your work and in everything you put your hand to.

DEUTERONOMY 15:10 NIV

Father, help me to see those who are in need and to be willing to give without hesitation. Show me how to love others above myself and care about them. You are faithful so I know that you will help me to easily show your generosity to all people and especially those whom you highlight to me.

Help my heart to be open to the stranger and my eyes to see others as you see them. Remove my judgments from me and fill me with the love that you have for all people.

You have given me everything I have, God, so I need not worry about giving to others. You are Jehovah Jireh my provider! I know that you will work within me to accomplish your desires on the earth. Continue to pour out your Spirit on me so that I can exemplify you to those around me.

Pleasing Fruit

"You didn't choose me. I chose you. I appointed you to go and produce lasting fruit, so that the Father will give you whatever you ask for, using my name."

JOHN 15:16 NLT

Father, I want to trust in your choices and to hear them. I know I need help to hear your voice and to rely more upon you, rather than myself. Give me ears to hear, and eyes to see, and that when I do find what you are doing, I respond with a willing heart.

Help me to produce fruit that is pleasing to you and accomplishes your will rather than my own. I ask that my heart would be given over to you.

God, you always make the best choices. You have all the knowledge, understanding, insight, and wisdom to do so. You have seen all that life can offer—good and bad and how it affects us as humans—but you are not limited by any power or dominion. Your power is unlimited and your ability to complete what you start is unquestioned.

The Right Place

The Lord is my strength and my defense;
he has become my salvation.
He is my God, and I will praise him,
my father's God, and I will exalt him.

Exodus 15:2 niv

Lord, I want a heart that trusts in you and worships you in all things. I say I want it because I know that my heart is not always in the right place.

Fill me with your Spirit that I may know your Word and your ways. I do not want to depart from you. I want you to be fully incorporated in my life. God, fill me with exultation for the great things you have done already and will be doing in me in the future.

You are my strength, God. You help me to overcome adversity and to stand firm in the face of temptation. I know that I can trust in you and praise you in all things at all times. You have my back, and you go before me. I am surrounded by your faithful, strong, enduring love.

Right Prayers

The Lord does not listen to the wicked,
but he hears the prayers of those who do right.

Proverbs 15:29 ncv

Father, help me to hear you and to ignore the voices of those who do not speak your truth. I know at times I allow for others to speak into my life because I fear what man thinks of me. Help me not to fear, but to speak and live boldly for you.

Give me what I need to show mankind your love, forgiveness, and righteousness. I pray that men would learn what it means to fear your name because of your greatness and because you hear the prayer of the righteous.

I know that when I pray to you, you hear me. Thank you for listening to my prayers and knowing what I need before I even ask. You are an attentive, loving father and you take care of me well. Thank you for removing wickedness from my life and giving me freedom to live without sin. Thank you for your mercy and forgiveness for the times I fail. You are faithful and just in all that you do!

Remain in Me

> "I am the vine; you are the branches.
> If you remain in me and I in you,
> you will bear much fruit;
> apart from me you can do nothing."
>
> JOHN 15:5 NIV

Jesus, I want to remain in you and draw from your Spirit within me. Help me to bear your fruit and to have an impact in others' lives that demonstrates your love and care for them.

I know that you want to draw others to yourself, so please help me to be a part of that process. I ask that the work and power of your Spirit would flow easily through me and be evident in how I treat others. Help me to be steadfast in my connection to you. I want to be wholeheartedly committed to seeking you.

You love all people, Jesus. You have so much to offer and a love that is so deep no one can measure it. You give to me daily sustenance, so I can pour into others' lives. Thank you for helping me to be fruitful in doing your will and bringing others to you.

A Mystery

Behold, I tell you a mystery:
We shall not all sleep,
but we shall all be changed.

1 CORINTHIANS 15:51 NKJV

Jesus, I love mysteries. Help me to desire more of you, to explore your Word, and seek you out to hear more about what you are doing on the earth. I know you want to share more with me about what you are up to, so I ask for patience to wait upon you.

Give me ears to hear you and excitement about what you want to show me. I am looking forward to your return and being with you for eternity, and I pray for the strength to make it.

God, you are gentle in your approach to me and patient with my slowness. You are faithful to get me to the finish line, and I know that you empower me to overcome my weakness. Continue to fill me with your Spirit so I am a testimony to you, and even in my failing, a witness of your mercy and kindness.

In a Moment

It will happen in a moment, in the blink of an eye, when the last trumpet is blown. For when the trumpet sounds, those who have died will be raised to live forever. And we who are living will also be transformed.

1 Corinthians 15:52 NLT

Jesus, I am excited about what you are going to do at the end of all things. I want to be there, and I ask that you would empower me with the strength you had: with the ability to endure even through death.

You gave everything to return all things to your father, and now I want to give my all to do my part. I need your perspective and I need your power, so please help me to trust in you for this today.

I will be transformed to be with you forever, Jesus. Thank you for your promises and creativity in delivering them. Continue to show me the great ways in which you are operating today to help me last until you return, or I am resurrected to be with you. I love that you have the power to raise me from the dead and I trust in you to do what you say you will.

Unmoved

Thanks be to God!
He gives us the victory through our Lord Jesus Christ.
Stand firm. Let nothing move you. Always give
yourselves fully to the work of the Lord, because you
know that your labor in the Lord is not in vain.

1 Corinthians 15:57-58 niv

Father, I want the ability to resist temptation like Jesus had.
Fill me with your Spirit that I may be able to see what the
enemy is doing and how to overcome it. You have given
me your Word to guide my steps, so I pray that you would
help me to adhere to it.

It would be easier if you just programmed me to do what
you want, but I know that you love me enough to give me
choices. Help me choose you at all times: to seek you and
obey what you command.

*Thank you, God, for your victory. You have provided me
with all that I need to do your work. You are faithful and
patient with me and you want to show me how to live well
and to accomplish your will. Continue to pour out your
Spirit upon me so I do not become discouraged by the
world and its difficulty.*

Daily Delight

You make known to me the path of life;
you will fill me with joy in your presence,
with eternal pleasures at your right hand.

PSALM 16:11 NIV

Father, I want to take daily delight in you. I don't want to have to wait until eternity. I want to know joy and peace that comes when I am given over to you. I have had it before, and I would love for you to do it again in my life.

Fill me with pleasure, so I do not seek after my own things. Keep me on your path so I don't choose my own ways. I know that I tend to get distracted with things that are entertaining. Help me to be captivated by you.

Jesus, you are enchanting. When I consider the way you made the earth, the creativity of your creation, and the work of your hands, I believe you have much more for me than I am experiencing. Thank you for providing all that I need to engage you fully, and for your endurance and mercy as you wait for me to get there.

Timing

"Now is your time of grief, but I will see you again and you will rejoice, and no one will take away your joy."

JOHN 16:22 NIV

Jesus, thank you for these words of reality. Help me to embrace the state of my situation and to not avoid the necessary suffering that takes place to prepare me. You know me and my faults, my places of weakness that need to be strengthened, so please empower me to overcome and endure.

Fill me with your Spirit to comfort me in my grief and to show me how to live when things are not going my way. Give me your words to say to others that I may prepare as many as I can for your return.

No one can take away what you have given me, Jesus. You have provided all that I need to make it through this life in a godly manner. I know there is no one else I can turn to that will do this with such kindness, patience, and love. I am confident that you are going to richly reward those who endure suffering in this life for your sake.

Dwell Forever

Splendor and majesty are before him;
strength and joy are in his dwelling place.

1 CHRONICLES 16:27 NIV

God, I am drawn to the power you display in creation. Help me to not take my eyes off you. I want to be overwhelmed by your love and captivated by your creativity. I know that when I can find complete joy and peace in you, nothing can set me back.

I love that you want to dwell with me forever. I also want to be with you, but I don't have the ability or power to make it happen. I need you, Jesus, to bring it all together.

How great are you, God! Your creation demonstrates your power and majesty. In you I know that I have a place of tranquility and I am well guarded. Your endurance allows me to be weak, your strategy allows me to be mindless, and your grace covers all my failings. But you have given me the ability to be strong, wise, and sinless. Thank you for fulfilling your promises.

About Your Business

Commit your actions to the LORD,
and your plans will succeed.

PROVERBS 16:3 NLT

When I am making a decision, I want my first thought to be, "What does God think about this?" Jesus, the reality is far from this, as you know, so help my mind and process to be re-oriented to start with you.

Waking up in the morning, I want to first think of you, and going to sleep at night, I want my last thoughts to be about you. If I could somehow do this, and my life was devoted to you, I would be successful in what I put my hand to because I would be about your business.

You have plans that never fail. You know what you want and how to accomplish it. I don't doubt in your ability to be successful, or your wisdom to know how to deal with a situation. You have the power to overcome any adversary. There really is nothing to stop you doing what you want except for your great love. Everything you do is laced with love.

Conquered the World

"Everything I've taught you is so that the peace which is in me will be in you and will give you great confidence as you rest in me. For in this unbelieving world you will experience trouble and sorrows, but you must be courageous, for I have conquered the world!"

JOHN 16:33 TPT

Yes, Jesus! I want your peace to be upon me. Help me to understand your teachings and adhere to them. I want to stick with them so I can live serenely and with joy. I know your confidence came from your relationship to your Father and your trust in him, so I ask that you would grant me the same depth of clarity and knowledge.

Fill me with your Spirit so I can live as you lived. I want to be a witness to those around me that even when I face trouble and tribulation I can overcome by your Word and your Spirit.

Father, thank you for sending your Son to make a way. Jesus, thank you for making a way so the Holy Spirit can dwell with us. Thank you, Holy Spirit, for being here with us so we can overcome and testify to God's goodness.

Always Looking

Give thanks to the LORD, for he is good
his love endures forever.

1 CHRONICLES 16:34 NIV

In a land that is dry and weary, God, I need to know your goodness. This world offers passions that quickly fade, but you have love that is everlasting. Fill me with your love and help me to overcome this world.

When I look around me, Jesus, I am discouraged by how fast I fall into sin. I want to be filled with your great power and fear your name. Put within me a heart of worship and gratitude so that whatever I face, I will be looking to you.

Thank you for your patience. Thank you for your faithfulness. Thank you for your joy. Thank you for your enduring love. I will put my frustration, my failure, my distress, and my dislike of things in your hands. I will trust in you to help me and defend me. Your love and your goodness will be a banner over my life.

With Favor

The LORD does not see as man sees;
for man looks at the outward appearance,
but the LORD looks at the heart.

1 SAMUEL 16:7 NKJV

Father, I want to understand the depth of your love for me. How is it that you look upon me with joy when you see my heart? I know I want to be drawn to you, but I fail. I know I want to seek you, but I am easily entertained. I know I want to always do right, but I sin.

With all this you still look upon me with favor, because of your Son. Help me to see that and be confident to ask you for your blessing, to ask for you to use me in your plans, and to be filled with your Spirit not because of who I am but because of who you are.

You are love. You have no limitations on loving me nor loving the worst of mankind. You just require the smallest amount of faith, and weak obedience to your Word. I have these and I say yes to you, God. You see my heart and take delight in my insignificant offering. Thank you for your goodness and love!

MAY

I pray that your hearts
will be flooded with light
so that you can understand
the confident hope he has
given to those he called—
his holy people who are his
rich and glorious inheritance.

EPHESIANS 1:18 NLT

Always Aware

Because you are close to me and always available,
my confidence will never be shaken,
for I experience your wrap-around presence
every moment.

PSALM 16:8 TPT

Father, I want to know your presence in every situation
I face. I want to have you close to me, so I don't fear the
unknown but am confident in whatever I face. Help me to
rest in you and allow for your goodness to surround me.

Whether I am in night or the day, in the darkness of despair
or in moments of bliss, fill me with your presence so I am
always aware of you. Help me to recall your Word and your
faithfulness to it.

*God, you are the one thing that makes me content. I do
not need any other love, affection, or pursuit. In you alone
can all my fulfillment be found. I trust that you will give me
what I need today to accomplish your will. You are with me,
and you will never leave me. You are my one and only.*

Precious Things

"For the eyes of the LORD move to and fro throughout the earth that He may strongly support those whose heart is completely His. You have acted foolishly in this. Indeed, from now on you will surely have wars."

2 CHRONICLES 16:9 NASB

O God, have mercy on me. I know that in my foolishness I have looked to other things to fulfill me. Yet, there you are, waiting for me to cry out to you. I ask that you would help me to turn away from the worthless things and extract the precious—the things you have for me.

I want to pursue the knowledge of your character so I can emulate the things you do. Continue to put in me a hunger for the things of your Spirit and help me to deny my flesh.

Thank you for your support of me, even when I do not notice it, God! You are actively looking for those whose hearts seek after you. You are not idle. I declare that you are good, and your ways are perfect. I enjoy who you are. My heart is yours.

Wholeheartedness

"I the Lord search the heart and examine the mind,
to reward each person according to their conduct,
according to what their deeds deserve."

JEREMIAH 17:10 NIV

Jesus, thank you for dying on the cross for my sins. It
sometimes terrifies me that my sins would be exposed. Yet,
you have taken them away and given me your Spirit. I want
to walk in a manner that is worthy of your presence in me.

I want to exemplify your love to others, and your suffering,
knowing the great reward I will receive. Pour into me
all that I need to love and pursue you in a manner that
demonstrates wholeheartedness.

*You are a just and good judge, God. You do not frivolously
mete out punishments on me. You are measured,
patient, controlled, and loving. Your heart and motive are
unquestionable. I love that despite my own inadequacy,
you are completely perfect. It demonstrates how great you
are, that you encourage a lowly person like me to grow and
become like you.*

Mustard Seed

"If you have faith like a grain of mustard seed, you will say to this mountain, 'move from here to there,' and it will move, and nothing will be impossible for you."

MATTHEW 17:20 ESV

Father, help me to understand what you want to do on the earth. You made it clear that if it is in your will, it is certain to happen. So, I want to have a faith this is aligned with your will.

Somehow, can you help me to listen to you and be patient to know what you are wanting to do on the earth? Give me more of your Spirit, in greater measure, so I can be confident to express your desires and accomplish your will.

God, you are a magnificent planner. Nothing that you set your mind to can be thwarted. I can know your will and I can walk in it. I am not so base as to have lost all familiarity with you; rather, I am being made holy so I can do your will and be in your presence. God, you call me holy, and you are sanctifying me each day.

United in You

> "If two or three people come together in my name,
> I am there with them."

MATTHEW 18:20 NIV

Wow, Jesus, you certainly have given us everything we need and more. I want to know your presence on a daily basis, and I know that you have given me your Holy Spirit to comfort me and give me truth.

Help me to go deeper into the things of you so that when I come together with others, our expressions and actions replicate who you are. I want to be united with other believers who seek after you and want you to be first in their lives. Help me align with people like this who are wholehearted for you.

God, you are with us always. Your promise was to never leave nor forsake us, and you have maintained that promise. Thank you for always keeping your word and for working with me to grow in my knowledge and understanding of you and the ways you work. I will continue to follow your ways and allow my heart to be inspired by your character.

Proven Way

As for God, His way is perfect;
the word of the Lord is proven;
He is a shield to all who trust in Him.

PSALM 18:30 NKJV

Father, you know my heart. I want to do what is right and follow your ways, but it is very difficult. There is more suffering involved in following you, more sacrifice of myself. Help me to demonstrate, as a proof, that it is worth doing what is right, and that it is beneficial.

I know so many who say that it is not worth the sacrifice, that we should just look to enjoy life. But you call us to love others, and that means we have to sacrifice ourselves. Give me your strength and purpose to love as you did.

Jesus, you were a willing sacrifice, not just on the cross, but throughout your life. You knew your friends and family would abandon you. You even knew at one point the Father would turn away from you because you took upon yourself the sin of the world. You took it all away from us. Thank you for your loving sacrifice.

Armed with Strength

God arms me with strength,
and he makes my way perfect.
He makes me as surefooted as a deer,
enabling me to stand on mountain heights.
He trains my hands for battle;
he strengthens my arm to draw a bronze bow.

PSALM 18:32-34 NLT

Father, you said you have provided all I need in this life
to be godly and to live a loving life. I want to pray this
Scripture with confidence even though so many times I am
shaken by life.

Be my strength. Be my guide. Make me stand strong in the
face of my enemies. Give me your power and your might.
When I walk out the door and face adversity, help me to
look to you before any other.

*God, you are a mighty warrior. You have the victory. I do
not need to fear anything except you. I praise you for your
achievements and the manner in which you work. Your
ways are mysterious, but you always come through. Your
faithfulness is evident in how many times I have failed, but
you have restored me. You fight for me and with me.*

Staying Power

"The Son of Man came to seek and to save the lost."

Luke 19:10 NIV

Jesus, I am lost. Many times, I have found myself wandering and wondering, pondering life and how I fit and how things all come together. Yet, when I do, it seems that you are with me, or seeking me out to find me.

Help me to stay close to you and not wander away from your precepts. Give me the staying power of surrender and sacrifice. I want to trust in you, Jesus, like you trusted in your Father and gave up all to do his will. Give me that strength.

God, I never feel far from you because you always find me. Even when I wander down dark and lifeless paths, your hand reaches out to guide me back to you. You are a warm fire on a cold day, a shining light in the darkness, and a cool drink to a thirsty soul. I love you, and I want to always be found by you.

All Aspects

Whoever is generous to the poor lends to the Lord, and he will repay him for his deed.

PROVERBS 19:17 ESV

Lord, you help me help others. I know that your eyes are drawn to those who have less: spiritually, physically, mentally, or emotionally. You care about me in these ways too.

Give me your eyes to see my own lack and how much you love me. Then, as you fill me, help me to pour out the same kindness and generosity to others as you did to me. I want my life to be an example, though minor, of who you are.

You are generous and your giving encompasses all aspects of life. It is not narrow, nor is it shallow. You have a depth of love and extravagance that is endless. You are the greatest philanthropist there ever will be. You know what each person needs, and you give beyond, pouring out your gifts and love uninhibited by our humanity.

Simple Things

When you live a life of abandoned love,
surrendered before the awe of God,
here's what you'll experience: Abundant life.
Continual protection.
And complete satisfaction!

PROVERBS 19:23 TPT

Jesus, how do I live this way before you? It is so difficult to be wholehearted in my pursuit of you. I know that I am pulled away and easily distracted. Help me to be disciplined so I can focus my attention and my passion on the things that matter to you.

I want my life to be abundant in you. Fill me with contentment: a thankfulness for what I have. Give me your love for others and a joy in celebrating the simple things of life.

You are so good, God. You have all that I ever need. Thank you for your kindness and mercy in showing me your ways and for saving me from my sin. You are definitely the one thing that I want to be my greatest boast. You help my life to be consumed with passion for you.

True King

"I know that my Redeemer lives, and he will stand upon the earth at last. And after my body has decayed, yet in my body I will see God! I will see him for myself."

JOB 19:25-26 NLT

Jesus, I trust that you will return. I look forward to the eternal presence of God dwelling upon the earth with men. I pray that you help me to be there on that day. I want to be counted with those who stood firm until the very end, awaiting, and fervently anticipating your arrival.

If I die, then let it be doing your work and living out your purposes in my life. Save me from walking away from you or fearing the loss of my life because I believe in you. Give me your strength, Jesus, to endure all things for the sake of the gospel.

Jesus, you will come to rule and reign on the earth. Your kingdom is not of this world, but it will become one with it when you return. You will establish yourself as the one true King over all the earth, and every tongue, tribe, and nation will bow before you, confessing your lordship and giving you the glory due your name. I do this now in preparation for that day. I only worship one man, the god-man—Jesus Christ.

It Is Possible

"Humanly speaking, it is impossible.
But with God everything is possible."

MATTHEW 19:26 NLT

Father, I want to believe in your miracles, and I want to see your power demonstrated on earth as it was in the days when Jesus walked the earth. Let me learn how to surrender myself so you are glorified in me, and my life is a witness of your love and mercy.

Help me to look to serve others and not myself, then, as I do what you would do. I want your power to be evident in my life and flow to others around me.

God, you are magnificent and glorious. You are capable, powerful, and willing to move upon your people and show your authority and might. Show us your glory, God! Let this be a generation that seeks after you with one mind, so you can pour out your Spirit upon those who trust in you. I will be one who trusts in you.

Forever Family

Once you were not a people,
but now you are the people of God;
once you had not received mercy,
but now you have received mercy.

1 PETER 2:10 NIV

Father, you have adopted me into your family. Give me your love, your kindness, and your mercy, so I can bring others into the family. No one wants to be around my prideful arrogance or my selfishness, nor do they want to know of my achievements.

People want your love and goodness that is in me, your care and concern for them. Help me to demonstrate that to others in a manner that allows them to see your character.

God, you alone are famous for your kindness. You saved all people through the greatest sacrifice ever seen—a Creator dying for his creation. Who does this but you? Then you called me into your family, and adopted me, lavishing upon me your love and mercy. Thank you for accepting me in my broken state and giving me a forever family.

Heart of Wisdom

Wisdom will enter your heart,
and knowledge will fill you with joy.

PROVERBS 2:10 NLT

Wisdom is found in the fear of you, in accepting that I am weak and need to know your ways. I want to understand how you work in me to make your intentions a reality. Give me more of your wisdom and help me to walk in a manner that fears your name.

Give me a reverence for a mighty God who deserves respect, honor, and admiration. I don't want to be found wanting when you return, Jesus. I ask that you would find me with a full heart of worship, joyful at your return, and excited about the future of your kingdom.

Who is there like you, Jesus? You provided a way to the Father through your own sacrifice. You give me all I need, and you continue to pour love into my heart and wisdom into my mind, so I can love like you loved. You provide for me all that I need to stand strong until your return. I will trust in your promises and keep them close to my heart.

Spirit of God

What we have received is not the spirit of the world.
We have received the Spirit who is from God. The Spirit
helps us understand what God has freely given us.

1 CORINTHIANS 2:12 NIRV

Father, thank you for your Spirit. I desire to be filled with
your Spirit so I can be a better witness to those around me
of your love. You comfort those who need you, and I know
that I am a part of the needy.

Sometimes I do not act like I do, but as I get older, I
understand how much I need your Spirit. Sustain me today
with renewed strength and passion for you. Fill me so I am
overflowing so others can see what you have done for all
mankind.

*Your Spirit of joy, contentment, and love is all I need. By
your Spirit, you show me how to live and love. I can trust in
the things you do and say to me. I know that when you ask
me to do things for others, it is because you love me, and
you love them. Pour out through me as you have done in
generations past.*

Vigilant Heart

If we are not faithful, he will still be faithful,
because he must be true to who he is.

2 TIMOTHY 2:13 NCV

Lord, you know that I am not a faithful servant. I need your help to stay true to your Word, and to remain faultless in my ways. If you don't show up, who do I have but my own weak self. Have mercy and save me, God!

Place in me a heart that is vigilant and devoted to your Word. Give me the love and passion that I need so I can endure until your return.

I know that you are faithful, God. You keep your Word, and your actions align with your character. You are good and your love endures forever. There is no one like you who does what he says and completes it fully. You are the only way to righteousness and life everlasting. I submit my brokenness and my faults to you; I need you to redeem me.

Pleasing Servant

God is working in you, giving you the desire
and the power to do what pleases him.

PHILIPPIANS 2:13 NLT

Father, I do want you to make me like your Son. I ask that
you would continue to do the things that help me to seek
after you and fully attend to your Word.

I want to be a faithful servant who demonstrates your
character, words, and deeds to others. I pray that my
desires would be yours, and my hands would do your work.
I want to be a servant who pleases you, God.

*Thank you for working in me and being willing to take a
broken vessel that you use for your purposes, God. Your
grace and mercy are evident in the fact that you are with
me today. You continue to further your plans with the use
of my hands, and I am full of joy that your presence is with
me. You are faithful and I will trust in you because you want
me to be successful with you by my side.*

Renewed Creation

The world and its desires pass away,
but whoever does the will of God lives forever.

1 John 2:17 niv

God, it is hard to imagine your renewed creation better than this one. There is such beauty in what you have made. Give me understanding that comes from your Holy Spirit, so I may consider its wonder.

Provide your strength in me so I can stand until the last day of my life, or until your return. Encourage me to persevere in the face of trouble and difficulty that is so common in this life and so difficult to overcome.

Father, I will put my hope in you to fulfill your promises and restore the earth as you have said. Your Spirit will confirm the wisdom of putting my trust in you. You will renew my commitment to accomplish your will, for I will enter your righteousness and be nourished by your promises. By your grace, I will stand in opposition to the call of the world.

Foundation Stone

God's truth stands firm like a foundation stone with this inscription: "The Lord knows those who are his," and "All who belong to the Lord must turn away from evil."

2 Timothy 2:19 NLT

Father, I pray that you fulfill in me your promises, to uphold me and make me like your Son. I am willing. Help me in my unbelief, God. You know the trials that I face and the desire of Satan to overcome me with trouble and temptation.

I know you are faithful, so I ask that you would help me to remain in your Word, to trust in your strength alone, and to lift my head to you in times of difficulty. I need you, Father, to be my protector.

God, you can save me from my selfishness, and you can open my heart to your Spirit. Thank you for sending Jesus for us all, but I personally thank you for his sacrifice for me. I love your mercy and your kindness. You continue to turn to me even when I have strayed from you. Your love is faithful and incredibly enduring.

No Longer I

My old self has been crucified with Christ. It is no longer I who live, but Christ lives in me. So I live in this earthly body by trusting in the Son of God, who loved me and gave himself for me.

GALATIANS 2:20 NLT

Yes, and amen! I am so desperate for you to come and dwell fully with me, Jesus. I look forward to when I do not have to deal with my flesh. Help me to be strong in anticipation of that day. What sweet relief when I am with you forever!

Now, as I am here, I pray for great passion and devotion to you. I want my heart to be fully alive in you, and for your life to be fully evident to all who encounter me.

You have set me free from sin and death, hallelujah! It is no longer I who live but you live in me, and by your Spirit I am kept for the day of your return. We will be fully united, God and man together, dwelling on a newly created earth without sin and sadness. I can't wait for that day, Jesus!

Wisdom to the Wise

He gives wisdom to the wise
and knowledge to the discerning.

DANIEL 2:21 NIV

Father, you said that you give wisdom generously and without fault. I do want to be wiser, mostly to know your will and to be able to accomplish it. Sometimes I wish you had just programmed me to do things right. It would have been easier, but I know you set me free to choose obedience to you, to show my love for you.

Help me today to listen to your Spirit, so I may receive wisdom with patience.

You are wise, God. There are no wasted words with you. You are generous with your knowledge, and you share with me your ways. You don't hide from me but offer me good gifts. You encourage me even when I fail and struggle to obey. Your love is unfailing and pulls me up out of my trouble. You help me to decipher right and wrong, and then you lead me along the path of righteousness.

Honor for Honor

> "Those who honor me
> I will honor."
>
> 1 SAMUEL 2:30 NIV

Father, I want to bring honor to your name. The hard part is that it is easier to act dishonorably than it is to be reverent. Sin comes easily to the idle mind, so I pray you would keep me busy with the things of you. Sin comes easily to the stressed heart, so help me to rest in you.

Fill me with joy so I remain fixed on your return and the promises that you have given. I want my hope to be in you, Christ.

God, your actions are honorable. You love well, you respect your creation, and you judge justly. There is no compromise in you, and you cannot sin. I will learn what it means to fear and revere your name, so my actions align with your purposes. As the author and finisher of my faith, you will complete in me your will.

Wait for a Response

If you call out for insight
and raise your voice for understanding,
if you seek it like silver
and search for it as for hidden treasures,
then you will understand the fear of the LORD
and find the knowledge of God.

PROVERBS 2:3-5 ESV

My cries for help are heard, and I pray that I would respond to your answer, God. I know there are times when I ask for something, but I don't wait to listen. Help me to be patient, to invest time in waiting for your response.

I want my life to be tied up in pursuing you. I want others to see that my life is bent on seeking after you in all things. I know there are some things I do well in this regard but help me in all areas of my life.

I love that you listen for me. Like a father watching over his children, you stand guard, watching my steps and guiding me in the paths that you want me to take. I am so pleased to be walking with you, God. Who else can make me into a better man while covering my mistakes? I am grateful for your grace and thankful for your faithfulness.

Living Stones

You are living stones that God is building into his
spiritual temple. What's more, you are his holy priests.
Through the mediation of Jesus Christ, you offer
spiritual sacrifices that please God.

1 PETER 2:5 NLT

Help me, Father, to make my body a living sacrifice to you.
I know I can worship you in more ways than just a song.
There are actions, thoughts, and desires that I can align
with your will; these are acts of worship.

I want to be able to say that in all things my life glorified
you, so I pray for your help, and in particular your strength.
I know that I fail on my own, but with you I can be built up
as a part of the body of Christ into a mature man.

*You make me holy, God. You have provided the sacrifice
through your Son, so my sin is forgiven. In Christ I am a
new creation, a living being, who is able to worship and
communicate with you. Thank you for your redemption and
making me a pleasing offering before you.*

Deep Roots

Let your roots grow down into him,
and let your lives be built on him.
Then your faith will grow strong
in the truth you were taught,
and you will overflow with thankfulness.

COLOSSIANS 2:7 NLT

I want my life to be deeply rooted in you, Jesus. I know that you give me your Spirit who speaks truth and comforts me, but at the same time I allow my heart to be deceived and distracted. Help me to wait upon you and to gather strength from your Word.

Sometimes, because of the weight of sin and the world, I struggle to be thankful and content. I want to be joyful and satisfied in you. I pray that you would help me to be rooted and established in your love.

Jesus, you are building the church, preparing for yourself a bride who is spotless and clean. When you return, you will have me ready to meet you. I know that in myself there is nothing of merit that would overcome my sin. However, in you and because of your sacrifice, I have been redeemed. Through your love I am being sanctified each day.

No Other Way

He will give eternal life to those who keep on doing good, seeking after the glory and honor and immortality that God offers.

ROMANS 2:7 NLT

I believe in you, Jesus. I pray that my life and my passions would exemplify the heart that I have for you. Not only do I believe, but I also love you. I want to do a better job of expressing that to others. Not just for them to see who you are but also that they would enjoy my experience of you.

When my heart is full, I want to overflow to others, and that can only happen if you are helping me on a daily basis. Help me obey one—you!

Jesus, you are the way, the truth, and the life. I declare with all my heart that there is no other way to the Father but through you. I surrender my heart to you, that you would be glorified in me. Thank you for making me yours and for helping me to be a better man. Thank you for filling my heart with love.

Step Up

"He raises the poor from the dust and lifts the needy from the ash heap; he seats them with princes and has them inherit a throne of honor. For the foundations of the earth are the Lord's; on them he has set the world."

1 Samuel 2:8 niv

Father, I want to do good and to be rich in good works, to be generous and ready to share with others. Help me not to see riches as something I need to obtain, but rather to give away what I have. I pray that your Word would dwell in me richly so I would know your promises and not strive for any other thing.

You are all that I need God, and I want you to remind my heart of that when it is distracted by this world. Step in, and step up for me God, because I cannot do this alone.

You are generous, God. Who else gives their life away, and then continues after resurrection to pour out love, mercy, and all good things upon broken vessels? You surely do raise up those in need, and I trust that when I am in this place, you will raise me up. Your love is always faithful.

Gift of God

It is by grace you have been saved, through faith—
and this is not from yourselves, it is the gift of God—
not by works, so that no one can boast.

EPHESIANS 2:8-9 NIV

God, I receive what you have given. Fill my heart with your promises and bring to fruition the Word that you have spoken over me. Help my mind to remain engaged in the things of your Spirit and to pursue you over my fleshly desires.

I know that my works will be burned up unless they are founded by you. Guide my path so when I accomplish something, it will further your kingdom. I pray that the gifts you have given me would replicate to others and lead them to you.

It is by grace that I am saved, not by anything I can do, God. Thank you for taking me out of my sinful lifestyle and adopting me into your family. You have saved me, and I am eternally thankful for what you have done. I know that there is nothing I can do to make myself righteous enough to attain my own salvation. You alone did it, and you continue to pour out your grace on me.

Unimagined

"No eye has seen, nor ear heard,
nor the heart of man imagined,
what God has prepared for those who love him."

1 CORINTHIANS 2:9 ESV

Lord, I am excited about what lies ahead for all who believe. I want my heart to be intrigued by what you are going to do. How will you make my eyes see better? How will my ears hear more? How will my experience of all that you have created be improved?

It is exciting to think about, and I want it to help me remain steadfast in my pursuit of you. I need the hope and anticipation that it creates to sustain me. I want you to sustain me and nothing else.

You love me, Father. Thank you for your generosity, that you love well, and you have far more for me than just my salvation. You fill my heart and my imagination with new things when I wait upon you. You are faithful to show me your ways, and you are patient with me when I am distracted. Continue to draw me to yourself God.

Exceptional

You are a chosen race, a royal priesthood, a holy nation,
a people for his own possession, that you may proclaim
the excellencies of him who called you out of darkness
into his marvelous light.

1 PETER 2:9 ESV

I want my life to proclaim your excellence, God! Fill my
mind with what is true, what is noble, with things that
are pure, with lovely things that are admirable. If you can
do this in me, I will be a peaceable, thankful person who
reflects your love and goodness to others.

I ask for your Spirit to help me to be filled with patience,
kindness, faithfulness, and self-control. I want to be a
witness to the extent that people praise you for what you
do in me and through me. That way others will praise your
excellencies.

*You do exceptional things, Father. There is no doubt
that you are marvelous. I look at creation and am in awe
of what you have made. From the great expansion of
space down to the minutia of a snowflake. Your greatest
creation culminated in making us, in your image and for
your enjoyment. I am a part of your possession, of your
kingdom, and I thank you for how you have made me.*

Devoted Focus

Praise be to the God and Father of our Lord Jesus Christ! In his great mercy he has given us new birth into a living hope through the resurrection of Jesus Christ from the dead.

1 PETER 1:3 NIV

Jesus, it is not hard to praise you for what you have done when I am focused on it. Therefore, I ask that you would give me devoted focus on your promises and what you have done in me. I want my life to reflect your great works, not my failings.

Somehow, help people see you in me: the mercy you have given, and the living hope I hold onto. I want my life to be a testimony to the great God I follow.

I praise you, God, for your great works. You created me, and saved me, making for yourself someone who continues to choose you over other things. I choose you, God. I devote my life to pursuing the things of you. Because of your promises and the hope I have in you, I will be fully redeemed on the day of your return.

June

"Whatever you
ask in prayer,
believe that you
have received it,
and it will be yours."

MARK 11:24 ESV

Faith to Ask

"Whatever you ask in prayer, you will receive,
if you have faith."

MATTHEW 21:22 ESV

Father, I definitely struggle to believe this, but when I understand it in the context of hearing your Word and knowing what you want, it is not as difficult to believe. If I am patient and wait upon you, I can hear what you are doing, and I can pray in accordance with your Spirit. Then I will see mountains move.

Help me to be patient, to listen, and to be faithful to pray the things that are in your Word.

Your Word is true, and your promises are certain, God. I can be secure in knowing that you will do what you have said and that if I pray according to your will, it will be done. I know that as I step out and trust you, my faith will improve, and I will do greater things. You are faithful, Jesus, and your love endures forever. I can be secure knowing this.

Free from Anxiety

"Remain passionate and free from anxiety and the worries of this life. Then you will not be caught off guard by what happens."

<small>LUKE 21:34 TPT</small>

Father, I want to be inflamed for the things of you. Bring fire to my heart and consume the dross that leads me to idleness. Pour out upon me your Spirit, so I am free from the traps of this world.

Burn through the cords that bind me and liberate me from worry and the matters of life that take my focus off you. I want to be aware of what you are doing and follow the actions of your Spirit.

You are my comfort and provision, Father. I know that you care about me, and because you do, I can lay my anxieties at your feet and rest in your goodness. Thank you for your guidance provided by the Holy Spirit who dwells in me. You lead me down the paths of righteousness for your name's sake.

No More Tears

"He will wipe away every tear from their eyes,
and there will be no more death, sadness, crying,
or pain, because all the old ways are gone."

REVELATION 21:4 NCV

God, you are good. In the midst of my tears and agonizing through the worries of this life, you draw close to me. Help me to hear your words and dwell upon your promises. Excite my heart about what is to come, rather than being steeped in what surrounds me.

Continue to give me hope by your Spirit, that I would endure until the day you return or take me home. I look forward to that day when only joy, satisfaction, and peace will dwell with man.

You are faithful to do the things you promise, Father. I know that in you I have assurance of salvation and a guarantee of life everlasting. Jesus, you made the way for me to be included in your family, and I am so thankful. Who alone is like you?

All Things New

He who sits on the throne said,
"Behold, I am making all things new."
And He said, "Write, for these words
are faithful and true."

REVELATION 21:5 NASB

God, I want to understand the power of your Word. I ask that you would help me to read your Word and to take it in. I want it to pierce my heart and make me more like you. I want the power of your Word to change the things that I cannot change.

Bring maturity into my life, God. Help me to see that you are active and making changes with the same power that you used to create the world. Give me greater faith in you and what you are doing in my life.

I believe that you created the world, God. By your word all things were created. I believe in the power that you have to speak into life something from nothing. You are awesome and majestic. There is no comparable person to you. You hold me in your hands and my life belongs to you.

Not Ignored

He has not ignored or belittled
the suffering of the needy.
He has not turned his back on them,
but has listened to their cries for help.

PSALM 22:24 NLT

God, you do not ignore my cry. I know how much I need you, and I cry out to you for your peace, guidance, and strength. Place in me the assurance of your promises and help me to be a pillar for those around me who need you.

I want to know you so I can show you to others. Help me to be sensitive to your Spirit today, so I can be used by you to meet the cry of those who are suffering. You use all of us to fulfill your Word, and I want to be part of that plan.

Jesus, you are the head of the church, and we are the body. You set your church as your present hands and feet on the earth to meet the needs of those who are suffering. Thank you for your Spirit who guides me to love well, beyond what I am able on my own. Continue to pour out your Spirit on me.

My Safety

My God is my rock.
I can run to him for safety.
The LORD saves me from those
who want to harm me.

2 SAMUEL 22:3 NCV

Father, I want to run to you whether I need safety or not.
Help me to see myself as you see me, the need that I have
for you, and how much better I would be with you than
trying to do things on my own.

I want you to be the lifter of my head even when those
around me tell me you are not with me. So many speak
badly of you, but I want to trust in you with my life. I
pray for strength to turn to you; use that example as a
testimony of your greatness.

*You are a fortress, a shield about me. You cover me, God.
You strengthen me to do the things I would not think I
could do, and you bless me with your presence through
it all. You answer me when I cry out to you. Thank you for
pulling me out the mire and setting my feet upon solid
ground. You are always faithful.*

Take Refuge

This God—his way is perfect;
the word of the LORD proves true;
he is a shield for all those who take refuge in him.

2 SAMUEL 22:31 ESV

Jesus, I want to fix my eyes upon you. Help me to always be led back to you. I know that my heart drifts away from the things of you, so I ask for your help. Be a shield about me and a refuge for me. I want the truth of your Word to permeate my soul and fill me with a sense of security in you alone.

I know I need to hold onto your promises if I want to stand firm against the barrage of lies the enemy speaks. Fill me with your Word!

You are the perfecter and finisher of my faith. In you I have all I need to stand firm until the last hour. Like Jesus, I am strengthened by your Word, and at peace because of your Spirit with me. You will continue to be my rock, God.

Good Shepherd

The LORD is my shepherd;
I have everything I need.

PSALM 23:1 NCV

Father, I pray you would help me to understand your ways.
Like a sheep, I wander aimlessly at times, grazing on whatever
is before me. Give me your discernment; use your crook to
steer me away from things that will take me from you.

Place me in fertile fields that will fatten me and make me
a ready sacrifice: a pleasing aroma to you. I know that you
want my heart to bleat for you.

*You are the Good Shepherd. You see the dangers around
me and protect me from them. You are a mighty warrior
who can overcome any enemy. There is nothing holding you
back from caring for me. You have the stamina to endure
an ageless war, but there will be none because you are
victorious. Great shepherd, watch over my soul.*

You Know

"Whoever exalts himself will be humbled,
and whoever humbles himself will be exalted."

MATTHEW 23:12 ESV

Father, you see my words, and you know my heart. At
times I think I am all that, and other times I struggle to
know who I am. Help me to look to you rather than myself.

I want to walk before you in a manner which brings honor
to you. As your Word fills my heart, I learn what it means to
trust in you, but I need help setting aside time to seek out
your truth.

*God, I thank you that you know my heart. You can justly
judge me, and I trust in your perspective. You are good,
God, and you understand the failings of man: our weakness
and propensity for sin. You have overcome this, and pour
out on me your strength, wisdom, and exaltation. You alone
are the lifter of my head, and I will put my trust in you.*

Future Hope

There is surely a future hope for you,
and your hope will not be cut off.

PROVERBS 23:18 NIV

You are my help, O God. I want my focus to be filled with the things of you. I know my heart gets distracted by life, but I want my soul to be satisfied by you alone. You have what I need, Father, and I desire that my life would be wholeheartedly given to the pursuit of the knowledge and experience of you.

I do not want to be cut off from your Spirit, and I ask that you do not pass me by. I want you to fill me up, Holy Spirit.

You have established yourself as the premier of all other gods. Your prominence over all the earth has been established from the beginning. There is no God like you, Jehovah! I know that I can rest assured because of your promises. You will do what you say, and I can trust in you. You are faithful, and my hope is rightly placed in you alone.

No Lies

"God is not a man, that He should lie,
Nor a son of man, that he should repent.
Has he said, and will he not do?
Or has he spoken, and will he not make it good?"

Numbers 23:19 nkjv

Father, increase my faith in your Word. Help me to live in accordance with your promises. I want to show the world that you are real, that you are true, and that you are coming back to us.

Give me your strength to empower others in the same way. As believers in your Word, we want to be a testimony to who you are. Fill me with your Spirit so I can speak the truth of your Word with authority and not fear man.

You are truth, Jesus. In your words there is no deceit, no manipulation, and no malice. Your words bring life, your actions are true, and your love leads the way. I know that in you I can find all that I need for life and godliness.

The Narrow Way

He restores my soul;
He leads me in the paths of righteousness
for His name's sake.

PSALM 23:3 NKJV

Thank you, Jesus, for loving me. I ask that you would help me to lean into you whether I am going through tough times, or I am being blessed by your hand. I know my heart turns to other things that I allow to fill me, and then my soul becomes troubled by those very things.

Help me, Jesus, to follow after you. I want to walk in your path, to walk the narrow way, and be ready when you return for me.

You are a good shepherd, and you care about my soul. I find you in the quiet places, in the stillness you meet with me and strengthen me. You give me good gifts and lead me on straight paths. For your sake, my life is preserved, and your blessing falls upon me every day. Thank you, Father.

In the Valleys

Even when I walk through the darkest valley,
I will not be afraid, for you are close beside me.
Your rod and your staff protect and comfort me.

PSALM 23:4 NLT

Father, the greatest fear I have is of what other men think of me or could do to me. Sometimes my life and thoughts are caught up with how to be ready to fight, to avenge, or how to alleviate what I may experience from them.

I have enemies I have not even met and others who are real. But you call me to be led by you, and I want to trust in you more than my own planning or my hand. Give me strength to lean upon you and not rely on myself.

You never leave my side, Jesus. Even when I fail, your forgiveness, love, and mercy are with me. Your heart is for me when my heart is turned from you. Because of this, I am drawn back to you. It is your kindness that leads me to repentance. I find peace in your presence and protection when I shelter in you.

Laid Bare

Why would I fear the future?
For your goodness and love pursue me
all the days of my life.
Then afterward, when my life is through,
I'll return to your glorious presence
to be forever with you!

PSALM 23:6 TPT

I love your promises, God! When I am overwhelmed, lead me to you. When I am fearful, help me find peace in you. When I am anxious, give me your prayers of thankfulness. When I am filled with rage, calm my soul with your presence.

I know that when I turn to you all of my sin and all of my troubles melt away. I am laid bare before you God, who else can I go to where I fear nothing and feel no shame? Please make my heart turn to you alone.

You are my future and my hope, Father. I am found languishing on my own, but I am never alone because your Spirit is with me always. You guide me, your presence is with me, your love pursues me, and I have no true enemy because of your victory. I am at peace in you.

All Authority

The earth is the Lord's, and everything in it.
The world and all its people belong to him.

PSALM 24:1 NLT

God, I wish I understood your authority more. With the earth being yours, can you not do something about the men that wickedly ruin others' lives? If my heart cries out for justice, how can you not want justice so much more?

Please come and punish the wicked, fill me with love for the needy, and help your church to be a place of mercy for the repentant. Bring the world into alignment with your kingdom.

You have authority over all things, God. Every knee will bow, and every tongue will confess you as Lord. It will be a marvelous day when you return to bring justice and fulfill your love for what you created. I am excited and fearful of that day, but I know you are faithful to bring me into your kingdom. I am not worthy, but you make me worthy.

To the End

> "Keep your hope to the end
> and you will experience life and deliverance."
>
> MATTHEW 24:13 TPT

Lord, you know my heart. I want to make it until the end, and I want to experience the complete deliverance of this body from sin. What a sweet release that will be.

I am excited about knowing what life will look like as we live together on a new earth. Help me to keep this promise and perspective in all that I do. I pray that I would hold loosely to the things of this earth, that they would grow dim compared to the anticipation of encountering your glory.

Thank you for your daily encouragement, Father. You regularly show me truth, fill me with confidence, assure me, and give me hope. I will put my trust in you to bring me to the end, where I will hear you say, "Well done." Your Spirit is with me until the end of this age, and forevermore.

Slow Down

Use patience and kindness
when you want to persuade leaders
and watch them change their minds
right in front of you.
For your gentle wisdom
will quell the strongest resistance.

PROVERBS 25:15 TPT

Father, help me to be patient. When I want something, I tend to go get it. It's who I am. Give me pause when I am feeling irrational and fill me with peace when my heart is racing to do, or speak, the wrong things. I know that when I turn to you, I slow down and sense your presence with me. I want this to be an everyday experience, so my life is a testimony to others.

People need to see you, Jesus, and the church, including myself, somehow have to be the broken vessels to do this. Help us!

Father, you love all people. There is no one that you hate and want to destroy. You want that all people would be saved. Yet, love is also demonstrated by justice because love does not allow for the suffering of others without sacrifice. You, Jesus, have been the eternal sacrifice for all sin. Thank you for covering my sin and that of the world. You will bring love and justice to the earth for all mankind.

Steadfast Mind

You will keep in perfect peace
those whose minds are steadfast,
because they trust in you.

ISAIAH 26:3 NIV

What great peace I have when I am fixed on you, God! Help me to do this: to fix my eyes upon you, Jesus. There is so much that I can be distracted by. There are many things that my heart desires, and my flesh partakes of, that lead me away from you.

I really would like for my heart to be consumed by the things of you, but I lack such discipline. Jesus, you walked with great discipline and knew the Spirit so well; this is what I want for myself, so I will remain steadfast.

Father, your peace is everlasting, and your joy is complete. There is nothing lacking when it comes to who you are, your character, your actions, or your words. You are completely perfect and trustworthy. Your glory and majesty will be exemplified over all the earth. You will be praised because you are the perfect leader and the one true God.

Trust Always

Trust in the LORD always,
for the LORD GOD is the eternal Rock.

How can I help myself trust in you more, God? I am a flailing fledgling, with no control over my life. I'm blown about by the wind, yet I pretend that I have control. I fight for it, and I squawk when things don't go my way. I peck at those around me, and claw at things I want, but none of it comes to me.

Help me to see my need for you, to turn my wings and be lifted by the winds of your Spirit. I want to rise up on wings like eagles and fly with you God.

You are trustworthy, Jesus. In you I find a peaceful place to rest. I know that you keep me steady and on the right path. You will always prosper me, even when I feel that you are far from me, because you are good and do good for those who love you and pursue you.

Light and Salvation

The LORD is my light and my salvation—
whom shall I fear?
The LORD is the stronghold of my life—
of whom shall I be afraid?

PSALM 27:1 NIV

I am afraid. I'll admit it to you, God. No one else needs to know, but you do. You see my heart and you see how frail I really am. It does not take much to knock me off course. Help me to place my trust in you, rather than building my own feeble fortress.

Give me your strength and allow me to see how much you are helping me to stand firm. It is when I look to you that I am strongest, so give my eyes a clearer view of you.

Father, you care about me, and you said that I should cast my anxieties on you. I will do this because I know that you are faithful and are able to take care of the things that plague me. I will place my hope in you each day. Because of your Spirit in me, I will be patient to receive what you have for me. You have good things in store for me because I love you.

Even If

Even if my father and mother abandon me,
the Lord will hold me close.

PSALM 27:10 NLT

Father, you have invited me to be with you. I ask that you would help me to respond to you rightly, that my heart would remain open and contrite before you. Make me pliable to your Spirit and continue to draw me to yourself. I never want to be held in a place of contempt with you, God.

I know that your forgiveness and mercy is what I need on a consistent basis, and I only find that when my heart is tender before you. Give me a heart that is affectionate and kind, rather than cold and distant.

You will never abandon me, God. You are for me even in my brokenness. You never fail in loving me because you are love, and you cannot deny yourself. You are true and faithful, God, and your mercies never fail. You draw me to yourself because of who you are and because you love so well.

Goodness of God

I would have despaired unless I had believed
that I would see the goodness of the LORD
In the land of the living.

PSALM 27:13 NASB

God, you know this is true. I can knuckle down in life and
get things done when I have hope and belief in something.
But when I despair, and I am failing in myself, I cannot find
the strength to live. You, however, give me life and hope. It
is because of this that I can breathe.

Remind me of your goodness in my darkest hour. Lift
my head and my eyes to look to you. I know I can be
encouraged if you help me.

*There is no other God apart from you. Jesus, you provided
the way to the Father, and through the Holy Spirit I can live
serving God and experiencing his fullness. I know that my
life is secure and that my trust in you is not hopeless. I have
great anticipation dwelling upon your promises. In you I will
find my eternal rest.*

Uncovered

If you cover up your sin you'll never do well.
But if you confess your sins and forsake them,
you will be kissed by mercy.
Guard your life carefully and be tender to God,
and you will experience his blessings.
But the stubborn, unyielding heart will experience
even greater evil

PROVERBS 28:13-14 TPT

Pray for me, Jesus. I know that you are interceding for your church. I ask that you would help me to be open with you and real about my state. I want you to find no fault in me, but that is false. I am full of sin, fat with iniquity, enlarged by my own self-worth, and protective of my pride.

Give me your grace to see my faults and lay myself at your mercy. Fill me with humility so I can be lifted up by you. Help me to give of myself to others and love as you love.

I love you, Jesus. You have poured out your life for my sin. You have taken upon yourself my iniquity and replaced my rags with the riches of your righteousness. You have redeemed me by your grace and mercifully given me life in you. It is by your sacrifice that I am saved.

With You Always

"Surely I am with you always,
to the very end of the age."

MATTHEW 28:20 NIV

Father, I want to believe in your promises so that I never sin again. That is truly my heart, but my mind and my body do not follow my wishes; they follow my will. At times, my will is determined to do things that I do not want to do.

God, thank you for your mercy; may it always draw me back to you. Thank you for your forgiveness, may it always cover my failings. Give me a heart that is devoted to you and a will that is surrendered to yours.

I will put my trust in you, Father. I rely on your mercy and your forgiveness. I know that my heart is troubled, but in you I find peace that endures. That will provide me the sense of serenity to overcome any disruption and sustain my faith until you return. You are good, and I can trust in your perfect leadership.

Good Plans

"I know the plans I have for you," says the Lord.
"They are plans for good and not for disaster,
to give you a future and a hope."

JEREMIAH 29:11 NLT

Jesus, you did it all for me. Now, I desire that you help me to do things for you. It's payback time. But I am aware enough to know that my attempts to do anything close to what you have done are pitiful. I want you to be pleased with what I do, and I want what I accomplish to further your kingdom and to last into eternity.

Help me to love others, to share your grace with them, and to build relationships that last.

Father, you are good, and your ways are perfect. You have good plans for those who love you. I love you and I know that you have included me in your future schemes. You are aware of all my faults, my gifts, and my person. Despite my negative traits, you take what I have and make it great for your kingdom. Thank you.

Unreasonable Love

The LORD gives strength to his people;
the LORD blesses his people with peace.

PSALM 29:11 NIV

Father, show me how I am included in your family.
Sometimes I feel so aloof and separated from others.
Honestly, at times it doesn't bug me that much. I am happy
doing my own thing. But soon after time like that, I realize
my own selfishness and need for others.

Give me your heart for people that I may bless them as you
bless me. Help me to be a strength and encouragement
to others as you are for me. I need you, Jesus. I am never
alone.

*You never leave me nor forsake me, God. Even when I am
in my worst state and don't want anyone around, you are
there. You have an inordinate amount of love for me. Your
love is unreasonable; it makes no sense to a human mind
because none of us would put up with what you do. Thank
you for your love.*

Reminder

"Then you will call on me
and come and pray to me,
and I will listen to you."

JEREMIAH 29:12 NIV

Yes, you are faithful to hear my cry. I need to remember this, God. I need to recall that you are listening and attentive. Sometimes I walk about, doing life without acknowledging you are there. But you walk with me and have given me your Spirit to guide me.

I pray that I would be reminded of this, that I would turn to you in all situations in my life so that when I do, you will make my paths straight.

I know that when I recognize you, God, you help me walk the narrow path. I know in my heart that if I trust in you, and lean upon you, I will find the right way to walk. You are a strength to me in my weakness, and your wisdom is what I need when I am foolish. You sustain me when I do not recognize I have fallen, and you lift my head when I am down. Thank you for your enduring love.

When You Seek

"You will seek me and find me,
when you seek me with all your heart."

JEREMIAH 29:13 ESV

Give me a tender heart, God. I do not want your Spirit to pass me by. I want to learn to buy from you gold refined by fire and white garments that cover my nakedness. Help me to extract the precious from the worthless and find what you want me to seek.

My heart is weak and tends to wander after easy things. Make me a devoted servant who is pleasing to you upon your arrival. Help me to make my house ready for your return so you are overjoyed by what you see.

You give me the endurance to last, Jesus. I know that it is by your will and your power that I am sustained. When I turn to you, you lift me up and give me all I need to walk righteously and with honor. Because of your victory and power over the enemy, I have full confidence that you will overcome my sinfulness and reckless heart. You will help me be devoted to you.

Your Son

See how very much our Father loves us,
for he calls us his children,
and that is what we are!

1 JOHN 3:1 NLT

Father, I want to revel in your love. Help me to see that I am loved whether I am doing well or completely failing. I feel like I should never fail, otherwise I will lose what I have in you. You may not love me if I don't do things right. But children are loved by their parents even when they fail, and if as humans we can be like this, I can be confident of your love even when I fail.

Remind me of this, Father, so I always come back to you. I want to have short accounts with you, but I also ask that you would help me to love sin less and pursue you more.

You are love, and you demonstrate this to me daily by the very fact that I am alive. You give me life, God, and sustain my faith walk. In you I have the endurance to last forever because you are faithfully loving and eternally gracious. It is your kindness that leads me to repentance, and I thank you that you are my Father.

For Its Time

God has made everything beautiful for its own time.
He has planted eternity in the human heart,
but even so, people cannot see the whole scope
of God's work from beginning to end.

ECCLESIASTES 3:11 NLT

Lord, I know I am blind to much of what you do. Open my eyes to see you more. I want to see the beauty of your hand moving in people's lives and in my own life. It seems that the world is so quick to destroy your praise, so fast to tear down the God that I love.

Give me your words to speak truth to their lies, and to iterate your heart of love for them. I want to have your patience so I can see how you operate in the lives of people.

Lord, you do great work and the ways in which you operate are marvelous. When I ponder what you have made, I am astounded by its beauty and mystery. It gives me great encouragement that you are continuing to create and move. You are actively working on my heart, and I am so thankful for how you are changing me.

JULY

He will answer
the prayers of the needy;
he will not reject their prayers.

PSALM 102:17 NCV

Come Boldly

Because of Christ and our faith in him, we can now come boldly and confidently into God's presence.

EPHESIANS 3:12 NLT

Father, you have made me able to follow your Son, and I want to understand how I can do that better. Fill me with your Sprit so I can walk in faith without fear of the unknown.

Give me your confidence, Jesus, to boldly come before the Father and ask for what I want. Align my heart with his, so that when I do ask, I am asking for his will to be done. I pray for the ability to have great faith that moves mountains.

Jesus Christ, you tore the temple curtain in two when you died for our sins. By your work, I am able to enter into the holy of holies, not because I am righteous but because you are. Thank you for your sacrifice so I can have relationship with the Father. Thank you that I able to do your work as a broken vessel because your Spirit dwells within me by your righteousness.

Richness of Relationship

I bow in prayer before the Father from whom every family in heaven and on earth gets its true name.

EPHESIANS 3:14-15 NCV

My family is yours, Jesus. Help me to serve the family as you would and to love them with your love. I know you call me to trust in you, and because of that I am able to give of myself and my possessions freely. I want to learn how to bow, to surrender to you rightly, so all I have is yours to use.

Give me your mind especially when it comes to earthly things, so my life is not spent pursuing riches, but rather the richness of relationships. Help me to love people well but not take responsibility for what you want them to grow in. Give me your wisdom to speak your words and encourage faith in others.

Father, thank you for the large faith family I have. You have gathered many to yourself, and I am a part of your household. You prepare a place for me and promise me that I will dwell with you forever.

Unlimited Resources

I pray that from his glorious, unlimited resources he will empower you with inner strength through his Spirit.

EPHESIANS 3:16 NLT

Jesus, fill me with your inner strength. I read about how you lived and walked the earth, and I am so impressed by your trust in the Father. Though men railed against you, you knew his care for you. Help me to live in this same way, that I would increase in faith and rest upon the assurance I have in you.

I want to know your power and your authority, to see it flowing through this broken vessel and pouring out healing and hope to those in this world. Show me your way and help me to surrender mine to yours.

Jesus, you overcame Satan and crushed him under your feet. You have power over sin and death. You are victorious and have authority over all things. I trust in you, and I subject myself and my ways to your lordship. You are King!

Great Affection

> "God so loved the world
> that He gave His only begotten Son,
> that whoever believes in Him should not perish
> but have everlasting life."

JOHN 3:16 NKJV

I do believe, Jesus. Help me overcome my unbelief! Give me the fortitude to stand in the midst of people and cry out your words of love and affirmation. Help me to be a witness to the world that you love them and that you died to set them free.

You gave me liberty, and I don't want to use it to do what I want; rather, I want to pour myself out as a fragrant offering that pleases you and completes your will. Show me the things I need to do to prepare myself as a testimony to your great affection for mankind.

God, you love so well, and I am pleased to be called by your name. Thank you for sending Jesus to us to save us from destruction. I believe in you, Jesus Christ. I believe in your death and resurrection for my salvation. I am saved because of you, and I am being sanctified by your Spirit each day!

Willing Spirit

The Lord is the Spirit,
and wherever the Spirit of the Lord is,
there is freedom.

2 CORINTHIANS 3:17 NLT

Father, I want to know true liberty from sin. I know you provided a way for me to escape every temptation, but my strength is not enough on its own. I sin every day. In my heart I do not want this, nor does your Spirit in me.

Fill me with your endurance and passion so my heart is drawn only to you. Give me your thoughts, and renew my mind with your Word, so I can ward off the words of the enemy. My flesh is weak, but my spirit is willing.

Thank you for your freedom, Jesus! You have given me all that I need for life and godliness, and I embrace it fully. I declare that there is no need in me to sin and that by your Spirit I am continually strengthened and considered righteous before you. In you I have all that I want, and I am content.

Wisdom to Love

The wisdom that comes from God is first of all pure,
then peaceful, gentle, and easy to please. This wisdom
is always ready to help those who are troubled and to
do good for others. It is always fair and honest.

JAMES 3:17 NCV

God, I want to understand more about your promises and
hold fast to them. I know that wisdom is speaking through
your Spirit, and I desire for my ears to be open and my
heart enlightened to the riches of your glory.

I am missing out on growing in my knowledge of you
because of my own impetuous behavior. I cannot wait long
enough, but I want to. Help me to be less distracted and
more disciplined. Fill me with your patience, with joy, and
with endurance. I know when I gain more wisdom from
you, I will love others better.

*Father, thank you for giving your wisdom without restraint.
You are happy to pour out your Spirit on me, and I want
to partake of the feast that you lay before me. You have
provided for me bountifully and I am full.*

Patient Preparation

"God did not send his Son into the world to condemn the world, but to save the world through him."

JOHN 3:17 NIV

I am saved by you, Jesus. I know this to be true, but I want more in my life as do you. It is hard at times to think about how little I have grown or changed. I get impatient with myself for not doing more, yet you lived for thirty years before beginning your ministry. In the meantime, you increased knowledge, faith, and trust, and this is what I want for my own life.

Help me to follow in your footsteps and then, when it comes time, to complete the great tasks you have for me. Help me also to be listening to the small things that you want me to be obedient in.

God, you are merciful and kind. Your love is evident all the time, and especially when I reflect upon the sacrifice Jesus made for my sin and the sin of the world. You are faithful and patient.

Joyful Singing

"The Lord your God is with you,
the Mighty Warrior who saves.
He will take great delight in you;
in his love he will no longer rebuke you,
but will rejoice over you with singing."

ZEPHANIAH 3:17 NIV

I am trying to imagine you singing, God. What does that sound like? I imagine the power of earthquakes, rushing wind, thunder and lightning mixed with a beautiful melody! It would be an awe-inspiring event, that's for sure.

I pray that the meditations of my mind and the actions of my will are pleasing in your sight. I want my heart to be devoted to you and the pursuit of knowing your ways. Give me your power and your patience as I wait for myself to mature in you. I know I get impatient, but you will work in me.

You are the mighty King who came down to rescue me. You have saved me and called me, and now because of you, I am made holy in the sight of the Father. Thank you, Jesus!

Sown in Peace

The seed whose fruit is righteousness
is sown in peace by those who make peace.

JAMES 3:18 NASB

God, make my heart peaceable and full of joy that I may overflow with hope by the power of your Holy Spirit. Help me to make peace with all who wage war against me. Out of my actions, and through the contentment of my spirit, I want to be a witness of your righteousness.

You are my hope and my source of life, and I want my mind to be set upon seeking you and not the favor of man. Help me to work hard at seeking you first in all things that I may bring you glory.

Father, you put your Spirit in me to glorify you and enjoy you forever. I praise you for the peace that you have given me and the assurances of your faithful promises which uphold me each day. You make me brave because I trust in you to fight for me and to help me endure.

Friends

"Look! I stand at the door and knock.
If you hear my voice and open the door, I will come in,
and we will share a meal together as friends."

REVELATION 3:20 NLT

Jesus, I love the idea that we are friends. I tell others who
know you that one of the things I am excited about is being
with them a thousand years from now. We will all be together
as a huge family full of love, laughter, peace, and joy.

I want to remember this each day, so I am strengthened by
hope especially in those times of darkness when all around
me is wickedness and suffering. This life is not worth
comparing to what is to come for those who believe. Help
me to get to the end.

Jesus, thank you for seeking me out and choosing me.
You came to my door, and we fellowship regularly. I know
your presence in my life, and it gives me great joy to be
strengthened by our friendship. You are faithful to stand
with me forever. I trust in you.

More Than

With God's power working in us, God can do much,
much more than anything we can ask or imagine.

EPHESIANS 3:21 NCV

God, I want your power working in me to a greater degree.
I know your Spirit is within me and working on my heart,
but I want more, and I want to see more movement in my
life on things that hold me back. Eventually, I want such
deep experiences with you that I would be full of love and
power to see others healed and set free.

Please continue to do in me things beyond even my own
imagination. I can imagine you doing some pretty big
things through me when I am fully surrendered to you.

*There is no limit on your power, your love, or your
knowledge. Nothing is beyond you, Jesus. You are
marvelous and my heart is full of praise for you. You
continue to work in me in ways that amaze me. You have
such grace and kindness, and my soul is glad that you love
me so much.*

Renewed Body

He will take our weak mortal bodies and change them
into glorious bodies like his own, using the same power
with which he will bring everything under his control.

PHILIPPIANS 3:21 NLT

Oh God, how I long for this day! My body is ageing, and
sin is rotting my bones. How great that you will renew me
one day into a body like your own! I pray for your power to
infuse my life, that you would concrete my faith and allow
this temple of the Holy Spirit to remain strong until the day
of my transformation.

Whether by death or your return, I am excited to be
resurrected and to know that you have things under
control. You can help me to stand firm.

*You are glorious, Jesus. Fully human and fully God, you
are seated at the right hand of the Father, praying for
your Church to be ready and endure until the end. By your
power and your will, we will all be saved in that day. You
have overcome and I will stand with you by the word of my
testimony and your blood.*

Testimony of Love

The steadfast love of the LORD never ceases;
his mercies never come to an end;
they are new every morning;
great is your faithfulness.

LAMENTATIONS 3:22-23 ESV

Lord, I pray for my faithfulness to match yours. Somehow you can work in me, by your Spirit, to purify my heart and keep me devoted to you. I want to rise with you each day and lay down each night with you on my mind. Fill my heart with unceasing praise for you, so I am not taken by any other love.

Help me to encourage others around me to look to you in the same way that my heart looks to you. I want to be a strong testimony of your love to all people but also a witness to the truth of your Word.

God, you are my rock and my salvation. It is by your Word that I am saved, and by your steadfast love that I can endure. I hope in you all day long and I am not disappointed by you. You are faithful.

Made Right

We are made right with God by placing our faith in
Jesus Christ. And this is true for everyone who believes,
no matter who we are. For everyone has sinned;
we all fall short of God's glorious standard.

ROMANS 3:22-23 NLT

Father, I want to walk in your ways. It is in my heart to do
your will, but I know that my propensity is toward sin and
the ease for which I am gratified by things of this world.
Give me a heart that hates sin and loves you. Fill me with
joy in your Spirit and passion for your Word.

I want to be like a tree planted by streams of your living
water, yielding good fruit in the right season. When
you help me, God, I know that I can be prosperous and
accomplish the things you have given me to do. I want to
further your kingdom.

*You are a righteous and holy God. You stand alone from
everyone and everything you created. You need no
justification to exist and no one to uphold you. You are
God, and I am your lowly creation: a simple work of your
hands. I bow my knee before you, mighty King, and I
worship your glorious name.*

Best Effort

Whatever you do, work heartily,
as for the Lord and not for men,
knowing that from the Lord you will receive
the inheritance as your reward.
You are serving the Lord Christ.

COLOSSIANS 3:23-24 ESV

Jesus, one day I hope to hear you say that I have done well and that I am a faithful servant. I know that to get to that point I must be patient, listen for your Spirit, and obey what he tells me to do. I want my life to be lived like that, but I am so far short of it.

Help me to find joy in doing your will and peace in the process of surrender. I desire that my life be yours, but I struggle to let it go. Help me to do your will and to please you alone.

You are worthy of my best effort, God. You deserve more than men can ever give, but you delight in the little we do offer. I love that about you. You have a generous, kind heart, and I am thankful for your love for me.

Sweet Sleep

When you lie down, you will not be afraid;
when you lie down, your sleep will be sweet.

PROVERBS 3:24 NIV

Father, I want your peace to pervade my place. Whoever is with me, and whatever is happening in my life, I want my home to be filled with your Spirit. I know when this happens my life will be filled with joy and contentment.

Fill my home with your Word, that I would meditate on it day and night. Help me to lead my family and friends to your Word. I want it to be written on my heart and adhere to it all the days of my life. Fill my dreams with your truth and grant me continued peace.

You are my hiding place, God. In you, I find all that I am looking for. Thank you for being present when I am asleep or awake. I know that you are near me always because you are faithful and true to your Word. You never forsake or leave me.

Wait Quietly

The Lord is good to those who depend on him,
to those who search for him.
So it is good to wait quietly
for salvation from the Lord.

LAMENTATIONS 3:25-26 NLT

It is hard for me to wait sometimes. I can sit for a long
time when it serves a purpose, and I know this is where
I struggle to sit and wait on you, God. I forget that it is
serving a purpose because I don't see results as fast as I
would like. It would be so nice to sit down and just shoot
the breeze with you. Why can it not be that easy?

Help me to search for you, to seek you out in the quiet
places, and to have endurance in my waiting. Give me your
focus, Jesus, so I can remain fixed on you.

*You are good and faithful, Father, and you reward those
who diligently seek you. You give good gifts, and you freely
give wisdom without restraint. You take my burdens and
make them light, and your yoke is easy upon me. I will seek
you and find you.*

My Confidence

The LORD will be your confidence
and will keep your foot from being caught.

PROVERBS 3:26 ESV

Lord, I want you to uphold me with your right hand. Keep me from stumbling, from falling and failing. Give me your eyes to see the road ahead and help me to have confidence in your leadership. I know that you see me going my own way at times, but I thank you that you gently lead me back to you.

Fill me with your Spirit and do not pass me by. Anoint my head with the oil of gladness so when I face adversity I can laugh in its face. You can and will give me the endurance I need to be sustained until the end.

Father, you bless me and keep me. Your face shines upon me and you are gracious to me. Thank you that your countenance is toward me, and you give me peace. Thank you for watching over me.

Victorious Conquest

The Lord is faithful;
he will strengthen you
and guard you from the evil one.

2 THESSALONIANS 3:3 NLT

God, I need your protection from the enemy. I know that my soul is a soft vessel, easily crushed under the weight of the world. I can pretend to be hard on the outside and strong for others, but in the dark of the night, when I am weary and alone, I cry out to you for your mercy and strength.

Uphold me and turn your face toward me, so I know you are there. Provide endurance to the angels you have surrounded me with.

You know the ways of the evil one, Jesus. You see his wicked scheming and laugh at his attempts to destroy your people. You are mighty and you have crushed death under your feet. You ride your white horse as a conqueror on a conquest that you will undoubtedly win. You are victorious, and I can trust in you.

Close Moments

Lord, you are my shield,
my wonderful God who gives me courage.

Psalm 3:3 ncv

Father, why does the world cave in on me so quickly? There are times of great satisfaction and joy in you, and then by tomorrow it appears to be gone. I long for those close moments where your Spirit fills me with joy and contentment. Like a deer pants for the water, my soul longs for this!

God, give me your power and your fortitude to stand in the face of this generation and speak the truth: truth loaded with love for others. Help me to know how to push back against what the world tries to heap upon your people. Give me your words and your wisdom.

God, you are my protector, and you cover me with your presence. I will find rest and peace in you. You wash my feet and cleanse my lips. You allow me to enter into your throne room unhindered and unencumbered despite the stains of sin and wickedness. You wash me clean and set my feet straight.

Covered by Mercy

No one is abandoned by the Lord forever.
Though he brings grief, he also shows compassion
because of the greatness of his unfailing love.

LAMENTATIONS 3:31-32 NLT

God, you can help me in my time of need. Your compassion is what I hope can save me from my wicked ways. I know that your discipline is there to help me, and when I am grieving my sin, your mercy covers me.

Continue to pour out your kindness on me even though it isn't merited. Forgive me for my sins and allow me to be welcomed into your presence. I ask that you would not leave me forsaken in my broken state, but heal me, clean me, and restore me to yourself.

You are a merciful God and a kind king. I am thankful for your compassionate heart and your love for the broken and contrite. You are the lifter of my head, a shield about me to protect me, and you clothe me with righteousness to cover my shame.

Not Working Alone

We are not saying that we can do this work ourselves.
It is God who makes us able to do all that we do.

2 CORINTHIANS 3:5 NCV

Father, how many times have I asked for your help? Too many to count! I know that I am not capable of doing all that you ask on my own. I need friends, and I need you. It is important that you help me to hear you through your Word, prayer, and through the body of Christ.

I am so thankful for those you have surrounded me with, and I ask that you would bless them. Continue to speak through them to me and help us all to do your will. I know that you long for unity in the body, so I pray for that to increase as we depend on one another.

You are faithful to make your promises certain, God. I do not have to worry that you will abandon me in the midst of something we are doing. You are there with me always even when I don't sense it. I will trust in your leadership and your good judgments.

All Things Well

Trust the Lord with all your heart,
and don't depend on your own understanding.
Remember the Lord in all you do,
and he will give you success.

PROVERBS 3:5-6 NCV

Lord, I want to put you first in the things I put my hand to, but I often forget to include you in my plans. When I have big things to do, I enjoy inviting you into those and seeking your wisdom. But in the smaller things I tend to move along without acknowledging you.

Help me to turn to you in all things, whether big or small, difficult or easy. I want my heart to be aligned with yours so I have a clear mind and I can gain your wisdom and insight. I want to be successful, so I ask for your assistance in all that I do.

I will ask you for help, God. I will call upon your name because I believe in you, and I trust you. You do all things well, so I know that my soul will be secure in you. You share with me your plans and provide wisdom willingly. Thank you.

Title

He saved us through the washing of rebirth and renewal by the Holy Spirit, whom he poured out on us generously through Jesus Christ our Savior, so that, having been justified by his grace, we might become heirs having the hope of eternal life.

TITUS 3:5-7 NIV

Jesus, I want to take in a deeper understanding of how your Spirit renews me on a daily basis. You have given us your Spirit so we can thrive on this earth, and I desire for more. I want him to teach me, to comfort me, and to help me grow closer to you.

I believe that he has been given to us to bring glory to your name, Jesus. Raise up in me a new standard of holiness and faith so that through my experience of the Holy Spirit, I will testify to your name and bring you praise.

You have given me new life in you, Jesus. By your Spirit I live each day with vitality and faith. I know that your Spirit was given so I remain steadfast until the very end. He will testify to my endurance and faithfulness—that I depended upon your salvation and not my works. He will testify that I made it by faith in you alone.

Repay with Blessing

Do not repay evil for evil or abuse for abuse;
but, on the contrary, repay with a blessing.
It is for this that you were called—
that you might inherit a blessing.

1 PETER 3:9 NRSV

Faithful Father, help me to not seek vengeance. It is very hard to forgive, and even harder to repay with a blessing when someone harms me. I know that by doing this you said I will heap burning coals upon them; perhaps that your judgment will fall upon them rather than mine.

Help me to trust in your all-seeing eye that roves the land looking to support those who pursue you and punish those who act wickedly. Allow my eyes and understanding to grasp the future of the wicked and to perhaps have compassion for them.

You are a just and loving God. One cannot exist without the other because love will not allow for unjust suffering, nor will it allow an abuser to go unlearned in his ways. Your love teaches and reproves. It gives a man wisdom and discipline. I trust in your love and justice.

Fast Pace

The Lord is not slow to fulfill his promise as some count slowness, but is patient toward you, not wishing that any should perish, but that all should reach repentance.

2 PETER 3:9 ESV

I am so thankful for your patience, Father. If there is one thing lacking in my fast-paced life, it is some slowness. I am not sure if that is why I am not growing as quickly. It is because I am too busy? I am continuously asking for you to move upon my life, God, and to make changes in me.

I know that it is not easy working alongside me as a broken and distracted human. I appreciate your kindness that leads me to repentance and ask that you would continue to diligently work with me.

You are so kind and so good, God. I do not deserve the mercies that you pour over me, but I will receive them with faith. Thank you for sending the Holy Spirit who comforts and teaches me. Thank you also that he convicts of sin, righteousness, and judgment. He keeps me on the right path toward my resurrection in Christ!

Not Idle

In repentance and rest is your salvation,
in quietness and trust is your strength.

ISAIAH 30:15 NIV

Help me, Jesus, to understand what rest in you looks like.
I know it is not sitting around all day contemplating life.
There is a season for doing that, but right now I know I
need to have busy hands that are not idle.

I especially struggle with this idea when there is a decision
that needs to be made and I cannot hear you clearly. You
know I act, so I ask that in your compassion and kindness
you gently intervene if I am taking the wrong steps or
thinking the wrong way. I want you to guide me, God.

*Soon I will have complete rest, God, when you have
returned or I have come to you. I look forward to that day.
You will be glorified in me, and my resurrected body will be
awesome! Thank you for all you do to strengthen me in my
salvation. I trust in you.*

Drops of Water

The LORD waits to be gracious to you,
and therefore he exalts himself to show mercy to you.
For the LORD is a God of justice;
blessed are all those who wait for him.

ISAIAH 30:18 ESV

God, how I need your patience. Show me your mercy again and again. I know that I need it, and I am aware of my many failings. Your goodness is like drops of water in a dry desert. Your kindness is like rain falling on a parched land.

I am desperate for your care and in need of your salvation. Pour out your love and compassion on me. Like a dam bursting forth and pushing all that man has created out of the way, smash my manmade sanctum, and fill me with your Spirit.

You are merciful and kind, Father. You take my brokenness and heal me. You ease my suffering, and you lighten my burden. You do not lay more upon me but share with me your strength and your Spirit. You are so good!

Like You See

O Lᴏʀᴅ my God, I cried to you for help,
and you have healed me.

Pꜱᴀʟᴍ 30:2 ᴇꜱᴠ

Out of the ashes I will one day rise victorious. Until then, I will cry out to you to save me from myself and deliver me from this wicked world. If I could see it as you see it, I am sure that my life would be different. My approach to sin and my understanding of others would change.

Open my eyes, Father. Help me to see like you see. Fill my heart with your hate for sin and your love for people. I want my life to reflect yours. I want my soul to be intertwined with yours.

You are my helper. Holy Spirit, you are near to me, and you comfort me. Father, you fill me afresh with your words and speak kindly to me. Your love is outrageous and lavishly poured out upon me. I can do nothing to earn more of your love because it is complete. Continue to answer my cry and heal me. You are my healer.

Blinders

When you turn to the right or when you turn to the left,
your ears shall hear a word behind you, saying,
"This is the way; walk in it."

ISAIAH 30:21 NRSV

I desire your guidance and your closeness, God. It would
be so much easier if you were close to me all the time,
whispering to me which way to turn. I need this from you.
I also want to experience you more regularly. I feel dry
and empty without your presence near me. Please show
me yourself and help remove any blinders that hide my
understanding of you.

Give me the Spirit of wisdom and revelation so the eyes of
my heart may be enlightened. Give me that incomparably
great power that resurrected Christ from the dead and use
it to awaken my soul.

*You are a good leader, Father. You have given me your
Spirit to guide me—the same Spirit that was in Christ Jesus.
I can trust in you to teach me, guide me, and comfort me in
all things. You are my close companion, my helper, and I am
thankful for your presence with me.*

Worth It

How great is the goodness
you have stored up for those who fear you.
You lavish it on those who come to you for protection,
blessing them before the watching world.

PSALM 31:19 NLT

Father, I want to learn from you. I pray that I would find
wisdom as I seek you out. I know that getting wisdom from
you may cost me all that I am and have, but it would be
worth it. Help me to believe that and to pursue it.

I know that the knowledge of you and your ways brings
about a reverence in men that I want in my own heart. I pray
that you would continue to show me how to live my life in a
manner that pleases you and brings a smile to your face.

*You are glorious, God. Your ways are higher than my ways,
and your thoughts are higher than my thoughts. I can lay
aside and surrender all that I am and I will be ok. I will be
in the right place because you are kind, you are good, and
you love extravagantly.*

AUGUST

I am praying to you
because I know you
will answer, O God.
Bend down and listen
as I pray.

PSALM 17:6 NLT

Source of Life

"I will refresh the weary
and satisfy the faint."

JEREMIAH 31:25 NIV

Jesus, you satisfy. I want to experience that more in my life. I know my own proclivities, and you know them better than I do. Help me to turn to you first for all kinds of gratification instead of trying to do things myself.

I want my life to represent you, but I know that I get in the way of myself. I humble my heart before you and ask that you would strengthen my weakness. Give me the power of the Holy Spirit to sustain and hold me up.

I look to you, my great and mighty provider. You are my source of life and contentment. In you I know that I can endure many things, and my life will bring you glory, whether now or in the end. You will fulfill your work in me and complete what you have started. The weak are sustained by you, and those who are faint and lifted up. You are my God and I love you.

Unfailing Kindness

"I have loved you with an everlasting love;
I have drawn you with unfailing kindness."

JEREMIAH 31:3 NIV

Father, I want to grow in your love. Help me to not only grasp it, but to also feel it deep within my heart. I pray that you would help me to receive your kindness. You know how much I don't believe you can be that kind. How can you still love me despite my failings?

As I get closer to you, I recognize the depravity of my soul, and I am humbled that you continue to show me everlasting love and unfailing kindness. Forgive me for my sins and cleanse me from all unrighteousness.

God, you forgive me of my sins. As far as the east is from the west, so you have removed my transgressions from me. I thank you that when I confess to you, you are faithful and just to forgive me and cleanse me from all my sins. You are faithful because you will always do it, and you are just because you paid the price, earning righteousness for me.

Go Before

The LORD himself will go before you.
He will be with you; he will not leave you or forget you.
Don't be afraid and don't worry.

DEUTERONOMY 31:8 NCV

Lord, I want to be brave when it comes to doing what you ask and bold to speak when you want me to speak. Fill my heart with your desire; help me to surrender to you and give me the words you want to share with the world.

As I read your Word, help my faith to grow and increase my ability to explain the gospel. When someone questions you, I want to be able to defend you. I pray for your presence to be close to me, close enough that I can sense you surrounding me in the midst of a dark world.

Thank you that you go before me, Jesus. You have poured out your Spirit upon all, but few have allowed you to fill them. I am one who is gratified by your presence with me. You have come to me, and I know that you will not let me go. I trust in your plan, and I give myself to you for your glory.

Effect of Peace

The fruit of that righteousness will be peace;
its effect will be quietness and confidence forever.

Isaiah 32:17 NIV

God, I long for peace, and I believe that my lack of it at any stage of my life is because I am striving within myself and not trusting you. Help me to understand my dependence on you so I would be full of confidence and peace.

Give me the Spirit of revelation and show me how you have set me in this place. I want to see what you are doing in my life. I want our minds to be one and my heart to be devoted to your desires. Fill me with a quiet spirit that is led by your Spirit.

Thank you for your righteousness, Jesus. You have set me free from the bonds of sin and death. I do not have to choose to sin but can decide to walk in the right manner. You have called me out of darkness into your marvelous light, and I am grateful for the peace and confidence this gives me each day.

Peace Abounding

"My people will live free from worry
in secure, quiet homes of peace."

ISAIAH 32:18 TPT

God, you know that my propensity to pursue things other than you lends to my worry. I get fixated on what others have, or what I don't, and I allow this world to cave in on my contentment. When this happens, I need you to remind me of the great things you have for me and the freedom you have given me from being enticed by this world.

I want to see more clearly the way of escape you have already provided. I pray that all who encounter my home, my family, and my life would find peace abounding.

You have given me security, God. You are my fortress and my safe place. You merit all of my faith. In you alone is my contentment and my sanctity. I find peace in you because of your great character and your strong, enduring love. You have my favor and my heart. I will worship you forever because you are worthy!

Hiding Place

You are my hiding place;
you protect me from trouble.
You surround me with songs of victory.

PSALM 32:7 NLT

Father, I know my life is in danger. There is trouble all around me. At any point, things could end, and I wouldn't have another chance to breathe, to see my family, or to show love. Help me to remember your protection over me. Give me the urgency to love others as you do.

I need to prioritize my life better because I want it to serve you and your kingdom. I am not always aware of your goodness and kindness in watching over me, but I do want to be better at acknowledging you each day.

You are a fortress and shield about me, God. I know that you have protected me many times without me realizing it. I love your concern and care for me. You have a hawk's eye that is sharply trained to see danger and avert it. You know the ways of the enemy and you save me from his snare. Thank you!

Teach Me

I will instruct you and teach you
in the way you should go;
I will counsel you with my loving eye on you.

PSALM 32:8 NIV

Holy Spirit, I believe that you speak to me in the night
hours. Help me to hear you during the day. Give me ears
to hear what you are saying. My life has been given to me
to bring praise and glory to the Father. Fill me with your
power and understanding so I can love others well and do
great things.

I want to walk in the manner Jesus walked and have you
close to me, so I can hear you guiding my every step. Lead
me in the paths of righteousness for your name's sake.

*You are a good teacher. Spirit of God, who dwells with me,
you are my comfort and my guide. You teach me the ways
of the Master. You lead me beside quiet waters and you
restore my soul. I find great peace in following after your
ways and living according to your Word.*

Resting Place

"My presence will go with you,
and I will give you rest."

Exodus 33:14 ESV

God, I want more of your rest. I strive to accomplish and to build up my name, forgetting that my life is to be lived for you. Give me your guidance and lead me in the ways that please you. Help me to search out these ways, to listen to your Spirit, and to be influenced by him in all my decisions.

I want to sense you at every turn, Holy Spirit, and I plead with you not to pass me by. Be patient with me, God, as I learn your ways and fear your name. I humble myself before you, acknowledging that you are supreme, and I am not.

You are my resting place. You give me shelter from the storm. When life rages around me, I can come to you, even in my sin, and find forgiveness and peace. I know that you will always be there; faithful and true are your ways. You never fail, God. Thank you for your goodness to me.

He Will Answer

"Call to me and I will answer you,
and will tell you great and hidden things
that you have not known."

JEREMIAH 33:3 ESV

God, as with all my relationships, there are times when I don't really want help, but I need it. Show me my state in these times and help me to see my own base nature. Forgive me for my pride and help to me see the things that are hidden from me.

I want to know you more, so you can share with me the great things you have stored up for those who love you and seek you. Give me endurance and patience to wait with strength upon your Spirit.

You are faithful to answer me, Jesus. I know in my haste I can lose patience and run too far ahead, but you gently pull me back to you. You hold me still for my own sake. In your ability to wait and see, with your knowledge and wisdom, you act with intelligence and reign with authority. You are a wise and understanding father.

Word Holds True

The word of the LORD holds true,
and we can trust everything he does.

PSALM 33:4 NLT

I find it intriguing that when I am in turmoil and my
life is fragile, it is because I have leaned on my own
understanding and trusted in man. Yet, when I turn to you,
God, my soul aligns itself quickly to rest in you. I want that
more, so I am not troubled by this world, nor giving my
belief to men.

I want my heart to be wholly devoted to you, not swayed
by man's opinion, and resolute in you. Father, you can help
me do this and live a life that pleases you. Fill me with your
light because your Word is true, and your ways are right.

*I know that you are good, God. Those who trust in you
and devote themselves to the pursuit of you will be richly
rewarded. You love when I diligently seek you. You give me
life everlasting, and you resurrect me to life.*

Rich Store

In that day he will be your sure foundation,
providing a rich store of salvation, wisdom, and
knowledge.
The fear of the LORD will be your treasure.

ISAIAH 33:6 NLT

God, I want to understand what it means to fear you but know your love. You are a holy God who deserves glory, praise, and magnification. I pray that my heart would demonstrate that to you and to others.

Give me a spirit of reverence and worship whenever I enter your presence. Help me to come near to you to listen, rather than blabber to you about the things you already know. I want to share my heart with you, and I want to learn to attend to yours. Make me ready for the day you return, and my salvation is apparent!

You will come back, Jesus. When you do, I will find a rich store built up for me. Things that no eye has seen, nor ear heard of. Thank you for giving me endurance and comfort. I will meet you. You will be my God, and we will dwell together forever.

Repentant Restored

The Lord is close to all
whose hearts are crushed by pain,
and he is always ready to restore the repentant one.

PSALM 34:18 TPT

Father, you are close to me in my pain. I know that I cry out to you often to help me because I do not know how to recognize your presence in the midst of my turmoil. You are already with me; help me to know you and sense your proximity.

Give me the right attitude, one of humility and contriteness. It is your grace and mercy that I need especially when I sin before you. I accept your forgiveness and ask you to help me mature. I do not want my life to be run by passions not directed by you.

Father, you are compassionate, and your love endures forever. I am thankful that your Son poured out his offering for my sins. Because of him I am made righteous, and I am justified in your eyes. In my humility, I praise your name; I exalt you, God above all other gods.

Radiant and Unashamed

Those who look to him are radiant;
their faces are never covered with shame.

PSALM 34:5 NIV

Jesus, in the process of sanctifying me, can you help me to look to you? I know that many times in my life I look to others to fulfill my needs. But you are the one who has it all—everything I need. I want that deep down in my soul.

I want assurance of your favor. I want to know that when I turn to you, all my needs will be met. Lead me beside still waters that restore my soul. Sanctify me with the washing of your Word that I would be presented to you spotless and blameless on that day.

When I look to you, I am beaming. You shine upon me and change my countenance. Like the sun after a storm passes by, I am warmed by your radiance. You have taken my shame away, and I am forever grateful for your kindness toward me.

Taste and See

O taste and see that the Lord is good;
happy are those who take refuge in him.

PSALM 34:8 NRSV

Lord, sometimes my mind does not think the best of you.
Or, I should say, I don't think I am of value to you. For some
reason, there is a block in me that says I could not be
loved by God. Help me to overcome that because I want to
believe that you are a refuge for me.

I need a place to go when I am in trouble. I want to find
goodness in the midst of this wicked world. Help me to
endure until the end. I want to experience the joy of your
salvation.

*God, you are good, and you love me. Even in my rebellion
and trouble, you reach out to provide salvation. Your love
endures forever, and there is no wrong judgment in you.
Everything you do is right and just. You lift my head when I
walk humbly and repentant before you.*

Prepare the Way

Say to those with fearful hearts,
"Be strong, and do not fear,
for your God is coming to save you."

ISAIAH 35:4 NLT

I am excited thinking about you returning, Jesus. It will also be a day of great trembling and fear. I want my heart to be ready and my body to be strong in the face of tribulation. Strengthen me to stand in this current culture and to learn what it means to endure.

Give me a heart that is not taken with the things of this world but is passionate about you. Like John the Baptist, help me to prepare the way for your return by straightening the paths and bringing truth to all men. You are coming soon, and I want to be ready.

Jesus, I am glad that you do not look upon my fear and weakness and label me as such. You call me forth and speak boldness and bravery. In you I do not fear the unknown; I am not afraid of men. I trust you to provide for me and give me what I need to endure until the end.

Mercy Seat

You, O Lord, your mercy-seat love is limitless,
reaching higher than the highest heavens.
Your great faithfulness is so infinite,
stretching over the whole earth.

PSALM 36:5 TPT

I am not a very merciful person, God. I ask that you would help me to be. I want your Spirit to fill me and flow through me, so I demonstrate your kindness to others. Help me to look beyond myself and my needs. Give me your eyes for people and assist me in looking for their heart instead of critiquing their behavior or appearance.

I ask that as you move compassionately through me, you would help me to be more willing to forgive. You have forgiven me and let go of my sin, so I want to do this for others.

You are a merciful and kind God. You have favor for those who walk in humility and seek after you. I am completely laid out before you when I think of all the wrong things I have done and how you have covered them. Who is there like you, God, who is so loving and merciful?

Caring for Creation

Your righteousness is like the mighty mountains,
your justice like the ocean depths.
You care for people and animals alike, O Lord.

Psalm 36:6 nlt

You have called us to be responsible for our planet, and you put the animals in our care, Creator God. Help me to be cognizant of my impact on the earth and to treat your creation as you desire.

First and foremost, I want to know how to love others better. You designed us in your image, and you will redeem us fully, but until then, help me to be a better man who serves as you did. I also want to care for the animals you created and honor you in how I treat them because you care about them too.

You are a just God who will call all to account for their deeds. You love well, and you demonstrate care to all of your creation. None of your creation was a waste, Father. You had a purpose and a plan for it all. Continue to change my heart as you are doing and bring me into the likeness of your Son.

Drink in Life

To know you is to experience a flowing fountain,
drinking in your life, springing up to satisfy.
In your light we receive the light of revelation.

PSALM 36:9 TPT

God, I want to know you more. I want the knowledge that
leads to godliness and a fear of you that teaches me your
ways. I humble myself before you and confess that I do not
understand as you do. My thoughts are not yours, and my
ways are not your ways.

I repent for my errors. Show me how to live and love.
Reveal yourself to me. Take the knowledge of you deeper
than my intellect; let your truth penetrate my very soul.
I trust that when you help me to know you more, I will
be satisfied and content in you. That is what I ask for:
contentment in Christ.

*You are good, and your judgments are perfect. Your light
brightens my soul and reveals the truth to me. I never have
to fear when I am with you because you care so deeply for
me. I will trust in your leadership and believe in your words.
You speak and fulfill what you promise.*

Every Promise

The humble of heart will inherit every promise
and enjoy abundant peace.

PSALM 37:11 TPT

Why is my heart so proud, God? Why do I resist you when I know that you are best for me? Quell the rebellion in my soul. I surrender my will to you. I want peace that comes from trusting in you and laying aside worry.

You have the peace that I want. It passes understanding, and when I have it, I can be thankful and rested. I long for the day when this will be my all-inclusive experience. When you come back, I want to be ready to live in peace forever. Help me practice it today!

Father, when I cast my cares upon you, I can find rest because you care for me. You are faithful in your promises, and I believe that you have provided all I need to live a life of godliness. I come to you in humility because I know that you will lift me up, and I will dwell with you forever.

Every Detail

The Lord directs the steps of the godly.
He delights in every detail of their lives.

PSALM 37:23 NLT

Father, I want to be godly. I want you to order my steps.
I want my heart to be bent on following your ways. Show
me how delightful it is to do your will. I recall how Jesus
walked the earth and loved to please you, doing only what
he saw you doing.

Help me to see what you are doing. Assist me in hearing
from your Spirit and being guided in all my decisions. Place
within me a heart that is passionate about your Word and
obedient to your calling.

*It is in your ways that truth and life are found. Only you,
Jesus, have the words of eternal life. You are the man that
brings man and God together, and through you alone do
I have salvation. I believe that you will cause me to follow
after you and I will find delight in doing your will.*

Stumbling

Though they stumble, they will never fall,
for the Lord holds them by the hand.

PSALM 37:24 NLT

Lord, I feel like I am stumbling through life. I guess that you are with me though because I likely should have been done otherwise. Perhaps your hand is nearer than I thought?

Help me, God, to see you moving in my life and to not be overcome by grief and stress. I believe you are faithful, but I struggle to see outside of my own circumstances and my faith is crushed by the defeats I face. Lift my eyes to you. Let me see your glorious victory in my life.

Though I trip and fall, your right hand is there to catch me, Father. Your strong arm lifts me in the depths of my despair. You never fail to intervene when I am overwhelmed. Your goodness is apparent to me in my darkest hour. It lifts my heart and encourages me to struggle on, knowing one day we will be together, and I will be forever safe.

Right Pursuit

Take delight in the LORD,
and he will give you the desires of your heart.

PSALM 37:4 NIV

Why do I purse things that are dead and lifeless when I have you, God? What is it about man that makes him so restless and disruptive? Why does my heart flutter for empty things that hold no promise and have no lasting impact?

Give me your passion, Jesus. Fill me with your Spirit. Invigorate my life and drive me forward to do things that please you. Help me to find out what pleases you. Expose the worthless things in my life and help me to extract the precious. I want to live for you and take delight in you alone.

God, you are worthy of my praise. You are creative, beautiful, delightful, enigmatic, joyful, and engaging. Why would I turn to anything or anyone else? You have given me your Spirit to encourage me in the pursuit of you and I will see your joy today!

Committed to Him

Commit your way to the LORD
trust in him, and he will act.

PSALM 37:5 ESV

God, I desire that my ways would be in your hands. Imagine being perfectly guided by the Almighty! That would be such a relief. It would make my life so much easier. If only I had the relationship Jesus had with you, Father. That is my desire; I just struggle to get there.

What does it take for a man, a person like me with a good heart but sinful, to really follow you like Jesus did? God, I want that. I want you to act on my behalf because my ways are committed to you.

My hands are your hands. My feet are your feet. My mouth is your mouth. Use me, God, as you wish to use me and complete your purposes in me. You are faithful to do this, and I declare that my life belongs to you. You are my delight and my joy. In you, I find my purpose.

My Hope

I hope in You, O LORD;
You will answer, O LORD my God.

PSALM 38:15 NASB

God, when I despair, can you lift my eyes to you? I need you to be the one who saves me. Anyone else falls short of what I need, but you are all I need. Please come to me and help me. Don't let the enemy overtake me; don't abandon me to myself and the wickedness of the world.

Holy Spirit, do not pass me by. If I am hard of heart or do not hear, break through in my life and change me. I give you permission to interrupt me. Crash in on my world, Jesus.

You are the only one who can save me. Jesus, you are the overcomer. You have demonstrated again and again your faithfulness and your ability to defeat any foe. I trust in you because of your promises that always come true. You are a very real presence in a place of darkness. You are my hope, God.

Priority to Serve

God has given each of you a gift from his great variety
of spiritual gifts. Use them well to serve one another.

1 Peter 4:10 nlt

Lord, you know my heart. I want to serve others, but I get
way too busy doing things in this life that don't matter.
Place in me a priority to love and serve others.

I want my life to mean something not because of
achievements but because I actually show kindness to
those in need. Give me your eyes to see the world as you
see do. There are so many broken hearts out there, people
hurting and no one to love them. Give me a heart for the
lonely, so I can share you with them.

*Father, you love those who are downtrodden and
overcome. You lift them up and encourage them. You are
the best friend a man can have. You speak love, truth,
and words of life. I find in you all I need, and through that
fulfillment you will show others what you have for them.
Show yourself through me, God.*

Humbled

Humble yourselves before the Lord,
and he will lift you up.

JAMES 4:10 NIV

Why do the nations rage? Why do people turn against you? Why do they hate your name? God, I want to be humble before you. I want to love you enough to speak against those who hate you. I want them to see your greatness, your magnificence, and the way that you love.

You have so much power and you could end my life at any moment, yet you do not. You are faithful, despite my unfaithfulness. I want to honor you above all others and glorify your name so all men will know how great you are.

Who is like Jehovah? No god can compare to you, God. There is none like you. No one has your power, love, and compassion. You are just and right to judge mankind and end us all. Yet you love and show mercy in hopes that we will turn to you. What a great God you are!

Living Word

The word of God is alive and active. Sharper than any double-edged sword, it penetrates even to dividing soul and spirit, joints and marrow; it judges the thoughts and attitudes of the heart.

HEBREWS 4:12 NIV

Lord, you know my heart. I ask that your Word would become alive to me. I pray that it would cut through the tough outer shell that I have developed. I pray that it would cut deep to the depths of my soul.

May your Word bring humility and repentance. May it bear good fruit in me, so on that day I will know your pleasure and delight in how I lived for you. Pour out your Spirit of revelation in my heart so I know the deep things of you.

I am glad for your rebuke, God! I am pleased to hear of the things I need to change to be more like you. It shows me my way and guides me in the right paths. I delight in your Word and love the things you say to me. Fill me with your Spirit of truth.

Participation for Joy

Rejoice inasmuch as you participate
in the sufferings of Christ,
so that you may be overjoyed
when his glory is revealed.

1 PETER 4:13 NIV

Help me to learn how to look to you in tribulation, God.
I know that when I see you, like James, I can bear even
death. He was full of glory as he praised you in the midst of
persecution. His life ended bringing men closer to you.

Whether my life finishes in that manner, or it lasts as
death slowly closes in late in life, I pray that you would be
glorified in me. Give me your endurance, Jesus. Show me
how you trusted in the Father and received comfort from
the Holy Spirit. Your faithfulness is an example I want to
follow.

*Jesus, you can sustain me through any calling you have for
me. Though I am fearful, you are brave. Though I may shy
away, you embolden me. In you I can endure suffering and
laugh in the face of tribulation. I trust that you will speak
through me at the right time.*

Endure All Things

I can do everything through Christ,
who gives me strength.

PHILIPPIANS 4:13 NLT

Jesus, Paul was an inspiration of incredible faith. His ability to speak the truth, suffer, and trust were impressive. How, from my current state, can you get me to walk in the same manner? I ask that you would show me how you will prepare me.

Give me patience to trust that you are at work in me. Help me to pray, to fast, to read your Word, and to fellowship with my brothers and sisters. Give me the faith that I need to stand firm as Paul did. Show me how to speak as he did. Pour out on me the same measure of the Spirit that anointed him, so I can do everything I need to do through you.

I know that when I walk with you, when I depend upon you, and when all my ways are committed to you, I will have faith to endure all things. You will move through me in amazing ways. I trust in you to get me there, Jesus!

Truly Motivated

"Whoever drinks of the water that I shall give him will never thirst. But the water that I shall give him will become in him a fountain of water springing up into everlasting life."

JOHN 4:14 NKJV

When I am thirsty, it is hard to think of anything else. My mouth is dry, my body is hurting, and all I can think about is finding precious water. God, I want my soul to realize its thirst for you. Show me so that, as when I am thirsty, I will doggedly pursue your Spirit.

I know that the key is understanding my state because then I can truly be motivated. I need humility, and I need your mercy. Pour out your revelation, God. Let your Word dwell in me and bear good works.

Your Word does not return void, God. It cuts deep and opens my soul up to you. Fill me with rivers of living water by your Spirit. You pour out revelation to those who seek you. You show your ways to those who are committed to you. I drink of your water, so I will live forever.

Without Sin

We do not have a high priest who is unable to sympathize with our weaknesses, but one who in every respect has been tempted as we are, yet without sin.

HEBREWS 4:15 ESV

Jesus, I love that you understand what it means to be human. You showed me how to live, how to suffer, and how to please the Father. I would like for you to move in me the same way, so my life reflects yours. It will help me to remain faithful until your return, and it will assist me as I share you with others.

As you have compassion on me, help me to also be kind to others. I want to love people as you did. You love so well because you sympathize with us. Help me to have compassion on those around me.

Jesus, you are the faithful high priest who knows our plight. You walked the earth and faced temptation and suffering. You know what it is to be human, yet you did not sin. Thank you for being righteous and for giving that righteousness to me. By your sacrifice and my faith in it, I am made right before God.

SEPTEMBER

"Keep watch and pray,
so that you will not
give in to temptation.
For the spirit is willing,
but the body is weak!"

MATTHEW 26:41 NLT

Day by Day

Therefore we do not lose heart.
Though outwardly we are wasting away,
yet inwardly we are being renewed day by day.

2 CORINTHIANS 4:16 NIV

God, as my life moves forward, a couple things are consistent: change and my growing proximity to death. These are sobering to me, and I pray that you would help me not to lose heart. I think of the change that seems to be always occurring around me, and how I feel like I am consistently trying to find a new normal. Perhaps it is my stage of life, but I know that from when I was young, life was constantly shifting.

I need you, God. I ask that you would give me the inner strength to be ready for the day of your return or the death of this body.

Father, you encourage me to struggle on in this life. You give me the power and the hope to continue. By your Spirit, I am renewed day by day even though my body is in decay. It is by your might that I am sustained, and I am thankful to you today.

Fit Together

He makes the whole body fit together perfectly.
As each part does its own special work, it helps the
other parts grow, so that the whole body is healthy
and growing and full of love.

EPHESIANS 4:16 NLT

Father, help me to see my place in the body and the need
for it. It is important for me because there are times when
I don't feel like being engaged in church, and I forget
that I need to for others' sake not just myself. Help me to
encourage others as they are placed in the body and to
enjoy how we have each been put together.

I know there are people I conflict with. Help me to embrace
compassion and acceptance and to see the value of each
member. I don't want to be unkind or dismissive.

*God, I love to think of how you work with me and others in
the body, to fit us together. You are so brilliant. You know
each of us and what makes us the best. You know how to
help me grow in maturity and faith, and I can trust that you
are using me to bless others in my role. You are a great
leader.*

Consistent Mercy

Let us come boldly to the throne of our gracious God.
There we will receive his mercy, and we will find grace
to help us when we need it most.

HEBREWS 4:16 NLT

Lord, you know me. You see my coming and going. You
know my thoughts and you search me out. I am not hidden
from you in any way. Forgive me for my unholy ways and
how independent I act from you.

Show me the consistent mercy you pour out upon me. Help
me to see how gracious you are toward me. It humbles
me to think that you are attentive to me in this way, and it
scares me that you see and hear everything.

*Thank you for your grace and mercy. You and I both know
I don't deserve it, but I am so thankful! You are kind. Jesus,
your sacrifice did so much for me, and I am grateful to you
for it. Your grace is sufficient for me to live each day in
victory. I praise you, God!*

Abide in Love

We have come to know and have believed the love which God has for us. God is love, and the one who abides in love abides in God, and God abides in him. By this, love is perfected with us, so that we may have confidence in the day of judgment; because as He is, so also are we in this world.

1 JOHN 4:16-17 NASB

Father, I want to learn to rest in you. Not only to rest, but to live in your presence. I want to be constantly aware of you in my day-to-day activities. Give me insight into what it means to abide in your love. I imagine it means that I have enough love that I share it with others.

I want your love flowing through me to others. This is how I would know that you abide in me. There is so much more you have for me. I want to believe in you; help me in my unbelief.

You are love and you demonstrated it in sending your Son from heaven to earth to die for me, God. No one can say that they know love if they don't know you. You are the clear definition of love and your act, the most humbling act of eternity, showed me love. Thank you.

Present Troubles

Our present troubles are small and won't last very long.
Yet they produce for us a glory that vastly outweighs
them and will last forever! So we don't look at the
troubles we can see now; rather, we fix our gaze on
things that cannot be seen.

2 Corinthians 4:17-18 NLT

Lord, help me to fix my gaze upon you. I know that this life
has troubles. You never promised it wouldn't. In fact, you
said it would be difficult and full of trial. You said we will be
hated, judged, and put on trial for your name. So, I expect
that life is going to get worse before it gets better.

Help me to be ready to give a good witness. Make my spirit
strong in you and fill me with the authority of your Word.
Holy Spirit, give me the right words to speak when that
day comes. I want to be prepared, devout, and strong for
you, Jesus.

*God, there is an incredible reward for me if I stand until the
end. You promise glory and an inheritance that I cannot
imagine. By your grace, I will be there to receive it.*

Stop Trying

Such love has no fear,
because perfect love expels all fear.
If we are afraid, it is for fear of punishment,
and this shows that we have not fully experienced
his perfect love.

1 JOHN 4:18 NLT

Father, it is very likely true that I have not fully experienced
your love. Help me to understand this. I think that you
love me, but I struggle with myself and my inadequacies.
Therefore, I labor to show how good I am, but never
measure up to what I know you want. You want me to rest
in your love, to abide in you, but I try hard to show you
how good I am, often to my own demise.

Allow me to receive your love through my brokenness and
assist me in letting go of trying to be right before you.
Even if I could show my good, it would not dissuade my
fear because you are perfect and holy. Help me to stop
trying and to accept you as my Savior.

*You are worthy of reverence and awe, God, but you also show
great kindness and mercy. I know that your love overcomes
all my fault, and I will trust in your salvation alone.*

Riches of Glory

My God will meet all your needs
according to the riches of his glory in Christ Jesus.

PHILIPPIANS 4:19 NIV

God, you are my God. I will seek you earnestly. My heart
and my soul cry out for you. Draw near to me and meet my
needs. Show me how much you are involved in my life and
the riches of all that you have for me to share in.

I depend on you more than I realize, although I tend to act
like I have it all together. Please continue to pour out your
mercy on me and help me to prioritize you. Show me how
to look to you instead of myself, or others, for fulfillment in
this life.

*God, your promises for my future are too valuable to
ignore. I look forward to receiving the inheritance I have in
you. I will be blessed by you even as you bless me now with
life. Though I may walk through the valley of evil, you are
with me to protect and guide me. You watch over me and
give me all I need.*

I Will Rise

For you who fear my name,
the sun of righteousness shall rise
with healing in its wings.

MALACHI 4:2 ESV

Jesus, when you come back, I want to be ready. I want my life to have been lived in service to your kingdom, in reverence of you, and in the fullness of the love you have for me. My heart needs your healing, my body needs your strength, and my mind needs the washing of your Word.

Holy Spirit come and fill me afresh and lift me up in the righteousness of Jesus Christ. You know me; you see all of me. Expose the hidden things in me and show me how to love you fully. When you return, all will fade away and I will rise with you.

Jesus, you have given me authority over all things because of your victory. You have given me healing and freedom from the fear of death. Nothing in life can hold me back from obtaining all that you have for me, and you are for me in achieving it.

The Greatest

You, dear children, are from God and have overcome them, because the one who is in you is greater than the one who is in the world.

1 John 4:4 NIV

God, thank you for your victory. I ask for your continued revelation of how your victory changes my life. I know you have saved me from death and hell. I know that you have set me free from sin, so I no longer have to live under its power. Now help me to walk in this belief.

Help me grasp what it means to walk in the power of your Spirit and to depend upon him for all that I need. I want to walk around like I have the greatest gift to share with others. I do have it, but I walk around like I don't. Please change that in me.

Your power and your authority dwells within me, Jesus. Through your sacrifice, and the gift of the Holy Spirit, I can live out my life as an example of you to the world. You have made me an overcomer by your Spirit within me. You are the greatest and no one compares to you.

Your Word

Your words have comforted those who fell,
and you have strengthened those who could not stand.

JOB 4:4 NCV

I want to read your Word and be comforted by its promises. When I read, Father, help me to picture your activity, your promises, and your work as it is happening. I don't just want to read words on a page, I want to understand what you are doing through and with your Word. I want to see how it is living and active.

God, I want your Word to be a comfort and a strength to me. I ask that you would remind me of it regularly. Help me to hunger for it, and when I don't take time to read it, to be like a person who is famished and cannot get enough.

Those who look to you are radiant, God. You are my comfort, and you provide the endurance I need to live in a wicked world. My hope is in your return and the promises I find in your Word. You reward me because I seek after you. You share with me your secrets, and I love you like no other.

My Requests

Don't worry about anything; instead, pray about everything. Tell God what you need, and thank him for all he has done. Then you will experience God's peace, which exceeds anything we can understand. His peace will guard your hearts and minds as you live in Christ Jesus.

PHILIPPIANS 4:6-7 NLT

Help me, God, to make my requests known more regularly. When I am thinking through a problem, or when I am making a decision, I sometimes ask for your help. But I want you to be involved in everything. I acknowledge that you are the one who guards my heart and mind, but it depends on how much I am subjected to you.

I surrender, Lord. I give you permission to speak into my life and to change me into your likeness. I ask that you would help me with my anxieties and those things that worry me. I don't want them to cloud our relationship.

You have the peace that I need, Father, and you never forsake those who trust in you. I know that my heart belongs to you. I can give myself and my life to you and know that I will be taken care of.

Growing in Love

Dear friends, let us continue to love one another,
for love comes from God.
Anyone who loves is a child of God and knows God.

1 JOHN 4:7 NLT

Father, I pray that you would help me to love others. I ask that you would give me a heart that is less concerned with myself and is willing to sacrifice ego for love's sake. You see my heart, God. You know what I am like and the things that I worry about. Take those burdens from me so I can help carry the troubles of others.

I know that fully receiving your love will enable me to express it completely to others, but I have to get out of the way. You are working in me a process which takes time and for which I do not have much patience. Help me be patient.

You have put your body together in such a way that encourages us to grow in love, God. You know that there are needs each of us have that can be met by one another. Continue to pour out your Spirit in me so I can love others with the gifts you have given me.

An Heir

You are no longer a slave, but God's child;
and since you are his child,
God has made you also an heir.

GALATIANS 4:7 NIV

Father, I know my brain has not accepted this fully. I struggle trying to serve you and work for you. Sometimes I am overwhelmed by that burden, so I end up doing nothing. Help me to see my place in you. Help me to rest in the fact that I am your son, and I don't have to do anything to achieve that. It has been done already.

I am thankful to you, Jesus, for allowing me to be adopted into the family of God. Continue to remind me of my status with you, the great promises that remain as I draw close to you, and the inheritance I have because of you.

Jesus, I am so thankful for your sacrifice that allowed me to be a child of God. Father, you made me your son! I am so grateful that you have called me out of darkness and into the light. I am pleased to receive all that you have for me.

Submit and Resist

Submit yourselves, then, to God.
Resist the devil, and he will flee from you.

JAMES 4:7 NIV

I submit to you, Jesus. I resist you, Satan, and I walk away from all that you offer. I renounce it by the blood of Jesus. I want to be free from the burden of sin, and I want to be bonded to you, Jesus. My heart is prone to sin and my will to rebellion, yet as I resist these and turn to you, I know you will help me.

Give me your strength and endurance that comes from dependence upon your Spirit. I want to take the way of escape you provide and be a faithful servant. Show me the way, that I would following in your footsteps.

Jesus, when you died on the cross, you overcame death and the bonds of sin. Through your sacrifice I am forgiven and made righteous. I am no longer in bondage. Thank you for your victory and the freedom it brings me.

Broken Vessel

We have this treasure in jars of clay to show that this all-surpassing power is from God and not from us. We are hard pressed on every side, but not crushed; perplexed, but not in despair; persecuted, but not abandoned; struck down, but not destroyed.

2 CORINTHIANS 4:7-9 NIV

I am a broken vessel that needs your healing, Jesus. Help me know deep within my soul your care for me when I am overwhelmed by the world. In my despair and my languishing, fight for me and give me your victory. Call me up and out of the miry clay.

Show me how to look to you in the midst of my chaos. I want the order that you have in your life even though you invited the chaos of man into it. Show me your plans and how you will overcome in my life. I need you to rescue me, God.

Despite me, Father, your goodness endures. Regardless of my hurt, your comfort never fails. You never run out of love and faithfulness. Though I go to the depths of hell in my sin and my brokenness, you chase after me and rescue me because of your great love.

Draw Near

Draw near to God,
and he will draw near to you.

JAMES 4:8 ESV

Father, I know that you want to be close to me. You are close to me, though I may not notice it. I ask that you would open my eyes to your proximity in my life. In most situations I fail to remember that you chose to save me and want me to be in your kingdom. Help me to remember this daily.

Remind me of the suffering you went through to allow me to draw near to you. I want you to be close to me, and I want to remain in you, that I would be brave and bear much fruit.

God, in you I have all that I need for life and godliness. You sustain me by your Spirit who dwells with me. Holy Spirit, thank you for your presence in my life: for your guidance, wisdom, encouragement, truth, and comfort. You are essential in my every moment and in my sometimes mundane life.

In Peace

In peace I will lie down and sleep,
for you alone, LORD, make me dwell in safety.

PSALM 4:8 NIV

When my heart is overwhelmed, lead me to the rock that is higher than I. When I am anxious and full of concern about my existence, give me your peace, Jesus. Help me to look to you in the most difficult times. I do not want my heart to dwell upon this life and the weak things it offers.

I want you to find me committed to your Word and obedient to your call. When you return, Jesus, I want to be ready with a lamp that is full and bright. I want to hear you speak over me that you are pleased with me.

Lord, you are my peace. You are the joy that I need to live each day fully. I know that your promises will come true and that you will return or resurrect me upon your return. My heart is at peace because of your trustworthiness, God.

Tended

He tends his flock like a shepherd:
He gathers the lambs in his arms
and carries them close to his heart;
he gently leads those that have young.

Isaiah 40:11 NIV

Good Shepherd, I need tending. Show me the wolves that surround me. I want to be close to your heart, and I want to make sure that my life aligns with yours. Guide me in your truth and lead me by still waters.

Help me sense your presence with me each day. I struggle to recognize the truth that you are with me always. I love that you shepherd me and my brothers and sisters in the Church. Fill us all with your Spirit and teach us to walk with you as you lead us. We need you, Jesus!

You are the head of the Church. Jesus, you died and claimed me as yours, providing me victory over sin and death. In you, I have all things, and I am specially led by you. Your command is my desire, and your will is my way. I submit myself to your leadership.

Bring Me Back

How can you say the LORD does not see your troubles?
The LORD is the everlasting God, the Creator of all the
earth. He never grows weak or weary. No one can
measure the depths of his understanding.

ISAIAH 40:27-28 NLT

God, sometimes my troubles are all that I see. Sometimes
my troubles overwhelm me so much that I ask myself if you
really care. I know that seems ridiculous when I consider
your character and all that you have done for me. But still,
when I am in a state of disarray, I need you to intervene
and awaken my spirit to your Spirit.

If you do not strengthen me, God, how will I ever be able
to make it? Please infuse my weary bones with your power
and make me alive to the things of you. I want to do your
will and follow your ways regardless of my troubles.

*Father, you promised me that you would be with me in
good and bad times. Your Spirit always brings me back to
you. Thank you, Holy Spirit, for being the hound of heaven
who chases me down, supports me, and lifts me up. You
help me look to the Father.*

By Your Hand

He gives strength to those who are tired
and more power to those who are weak.

ISAIAH 40:29 NCV

Father, I am weak and weary. I am overwhelmed by the
drag of life. When I pursue the things of this world, I am
like a man who carries rocks in a sack to deliver them to an
unknown place. Like a man digging and hole and filling it
back up again

There is no end game in taking delight in the things of this
world because they never satisfy me. Fill me with your
Spirit and with a hunger for things of you. Overcome my
weakness and overshadow my fears. Be my strongest love
and greatest passion.

*You are exhausting in your chase. You never give up on me.
I cannot hide from you, God. I love that you are relentlessly
loving, unchanging, and all-knowing. I am sure of my
salvation in you, and I know that by your hand I will enter
into eternity with you.*

Source of Strength

Those who wait for the LORD shall renew their strength,
they shall mount up with wings like eagles,
they shall run and not be weary,
they shall walk and not faint.

ISAIAH 40:31 NRSV

Jesus, I understand that you are my source of strength. Mentally it makes sense to me; however, when push comes to shove, my tendency is to run to other things to help me get through life. Please forgive me for when I have done this.

Help me leave behind the things of this world and cleave to you. I know that you want all of my heart, my desires, and my affections. Make me wholeheartedly yours. Fill me with your Spirit and enable me to make a stand for you that I may be irrefutably yours.

God, you are my salvation and my strong fortress. I know that when I am in trouble, or overwhelmed, I can run to you and be saved. I love that you have open arms for me when I do. You pick me up, and you destroy my enemies. You are a mighty warrior that none can defeat.

It Stands Forever

The grass withers, the flower fades,
but the word of our God stands forever.

ISAIAH 40:8 NASB

Father, thank you that I have the words of Jesus. I pray that you would open up my mind to receive what you have to say, and I ask that it would go deep into my soul. Cut through the tough skin I have, the fatty tissue and bone, and get to my heart.

Transform me by the power of your Spirit and fill me with the truth. Enable me to do as Jesus did, to walk in passionate obedience to the Father. I need you more than I know, and I ask that you would help me not to wither away but to stand strong for your kingdom.

You alone are King! You, God, stand above all other gods. Who fashioned man, and who made the earth? You did. You spoke it into being. You didn't even have to work hard to make it happen. Simply by your word it existed. By your Word I came into existence, and I praise you!

Consider the Poor

Happy are those who consider the poor;
the Lord delivers them in the day of trouble.

PSALM 41:1 NRSV

Father, help me to be more considerate of those in need. You have called us to love one another. To love you and to love man—these are your greatest commandments. I know that I need you to work in my heart to make that happen better.

It is easy for me to separate myself from others and just exist. But you want me to take on the responsibility of caring for those who cannot care for themselves. To give to those who cannot provide for themselves. Help me know how to do that wisely, without judgment, and with love. I don't want to enable others, but I do want to love them into truth.

God, you have given so much more to me than I will ever make sense of. I have such a great inheritance that there is nothing I need apart from what you have for me. Why do I need to look anywhere else? You are my source of life and provision.

Enabled to Endure

Don't be afraid, for I am with you.
Don't be discouraged, for I am your God.
I will strengthen you and help you.
I will hold you up with my victorious right hand.

ISAIAH 41:10 NLT

God, you are my God. I want to seek you earnestly. My heart and my soul cry out for you desperately. If only I knew the gravity of missing out on seeking you like you want me to. I think I may be surprised by what you have for me if I could demonstrate more discipline.

Give me your strength, longevity, and sustenance. When you provide for me, I am enabled to endure, but when I am distracted and amiss, I quickly fail. Father, forgive me for my sin and encourage my heart to chase after you. I want to have a drive to experience you like Jesus did.

God, you do not despise the brokenhearted. You love the humble and strengthen the weak. You heart beats for the lonely, and you have great compassion on all who come humbly before you. You love me with an amazing love.

Marked Forever

Because of my integrity you uphold me
and set me in your presence forever.

PSALM 41:12 NIV

Lord, you know I love integrity. But how much can I
consider myself a man of integrity when my heart hides
so many things? Enable me to face the hidden secrets of
my heart, so I can work on them in the light. I do not want
to be apart from you, but I know that my sin separates us.
Thank you for your forgiveness.

Continue to make me holy by your blood, Jesus, and fill me
with your Holy Spirit, so I can be marked forever as yours. I
do not want to arrive at the day of my judgment and have
fallen short of your love.

*Father, you never send anyone away who comes to you. I
was bound to death. I was alone in my sin, and my soul was
destined for hell. But you came down and rescued me! You
paid my price and redeemed me! Thank you, God, for your
salvation. Thank you for the freedom I have in Christ.*

Unstoppable

"I know that you can do anything,
and no one can stop you."

JOB 42:2 NLT

Jesus, when I read about your life and I see how you
walked, I have so many questions. What was it like for
you growing up? I know you entered ministry later, and I
wonder if that is the same for me. I know you are present
with me, as the Holy Spirit who dwelled in you is in me.

I ask that you would guide me in the ways you walked,
so I would be ready to do what I need to advance your
kingdom. Help me listen to your Spirit and be in your Word
and prayer regularly. I want to be connected to you, God.

*Lord, you are mighty and wonderful. When I dwell upon
who you are and what you are doing in the earth, I marvel
at your capabilities. You are the one person I think about
the most. You are my idol. I will follow you to my grave and
I look forward to being resurrected to be with you forever.*

God of My Life

By day the LORD directs his love,
at night his song is with me—
a prayer to the God of my life.

PSALM 42:8 NIV

I need your presence, Spirit of God. I want you to comfort me in the night hour, and to strengthen me during the day. Forgive me when I trespass against you and wash me clean. Wipe away the tears from my eyes, the dirt off my feet, and the thoughts of fear in my mind.

Fill my heart with overwhelming love for you. Give me a passion like that of the young man pursuing his bride-to-be. Help me set aside the things of this life that so easily entangle me and run after you with endurance. You can lift me up when I'm down. Help me.

Lord, you are so close to me I can feel it. I know that your love for me is never failing. It will never fade; it will remain steadfast regardless of my state. You are so faithful and loving. Your compassion never fails. You are the God of my life.

Only One

"Fear not, for I have redeemed you;
I have called you by name, you are mine."

ISAIAH 43:1 ESV

You are the only one I need, Jesus. When fear surrounds me, be my rock. When I am overwhelmed, cover me with your love. Take my heart and make it yours, God. Please, Spirit of God, draw close to me and help me to never leave you.

I know my heart is easily distracted and drawn away by the things of this life. You, the one I need, patiently wait for me to return. Come after me. Do not let me go down the road that leads to destruction. Make me yours alone and fill me with your presence.

Lord, you are my redeemer. I was destined for destruction, but you came down and rescued me! How marvelous are your ways. You astound me with your wisdom. I am so grateful for your salvation and your continued love for me. Why does anyone try to escape you? You are so good, and your leadership is perfect. I submit my life to your lordship.

Make a Way

"I am about to do something new.
See, I have already begun! Do you not see it?
I will make a pathway through the wilderness.
I will create rivers in the dry wasteland."

ISAIAH 43:19 NLT

Father, you have to help me. My heart is so darkened by
this life. I am tainted by the wickedness of this world,
languishing in life to the point of despair. Why are you so
downcast my soul, why are you in turmoil within me?

I look to you, God. Lift my eyes to you at this time. Help me
to see you actively involved in my life and the lives around
me. This is too much to bear on my own. Without you I
will fall into a pit and never get out. I cannot escape the
trap the enemy has set for me, and I am burdened beyond
buoyancy. I am sinking. I need you, God. Please come and
rescue me.

*Jesus, my rescuer, my Savior, you are doing things that I
cannot see. You are making new paths for me to walk. I will
be safe in you. I will not be overcome but will have victory
because of you. There is no mountain I cannot climb, no
enemy I cannot defeat when I am with you. You give me
strength to go another day.*

Calm the Storm

"When you pass through the waters, I will be with you;
and when you pass through the rivers,
they will not sweep over you.
When you walk through the fire, you will not be burned;
the flames will not set you ablaze."

ISAIAH 43:2 NIV

How precious you are to me, God. I need your comfort today. My soul is grieving, and my heart is weary. You know my state and what I need. I ask that you would take this life and make it yours. I pray that my heart would receive your promises and that I would rise on wings like eagles.

I want to rest in you, Father. I want my heart to be at peace like that of the disciples when you came and calmed the storm. Show me your ways and lead me in the paths of righteousness for your name's sake. I want to follow after you.

You are with me always, God. I remember this and I am comforted. Your presence warms my heart on cold nights and guides me on dark days. I find peace in you alone, for there is no other that gives my soul rest and allows me to trust completely. I believe in you, Jesus.

OCTOBER

Answer me when I pray to you,
my God who does what is right.
Make things easier for me
when I am in trouble.
Have mercy on me
and hear my prayer.

PSALM 4:1 NCV

Swept Away

"I have swept away offences like a cloud,
your sins like the morning mist.
Return to me, for I have redeemed you."

ISAIAH 44:22 NIV

Father, I am so thankful that you have accepted me into your family. You know my sins and my way of life. I am amazed at your grace when I sit and ponder how I act, my heart's desires, and the many things I have done wrong. I know there are several sins I have committed unknowingly. You even cover those.

I need your grace to continue. I acknowledge today that I am at your mercy. I pray for your continued forgiveness, and I humble myself at your feet. I am not worthy to be called a child of yours. I recognize in myself that I am completely depraved, bereft of any merit apart from the saving act of Jesus Christ.

God, you have redeemed me and called me by name. You knew me and spoke life into my bones. You brought me out of darkness into your light. Because of your sacrifice, I have been purchased. My life belongs to you. I am yours.

Hidden Treasures

I will give you hidden treasures,
riches stored in secret places,
so that you may know that I am the LORD,
the God of Israel, who summons you by name.

ISAIAH 45:3 NIV

Lord, it is tough to not be entertained by the things
of this life. I know that my desire for exploration and
entertainment can lead me astray. Help me to seek after
the secret things that you want to share with me.

In my heart I desire to pursue you and know peace, but in
actuality, I chase after things that lead me to destruction.
Give me your wisdom and pour into me your Spirit. I want
my heart to be intrigued by you again. I want to discover
your hidden treasures.

*God, you come to those who seek you out. You hide
yourself to be found. You love to give to those who are
poor. The humble are the ones who are lifted up. The
broken hearted are made whole. You are the God of the
man who does not love his life but gives it up for you.*

Ever-present Help

God is our refuge and strength,
an ever-present help in trouble.

PSALM 46:1 NIV

In my life there are a few things that I may say are my strengths. One of them is you, God. I do rely on you in some ways but not enough. I know there are significant and implicating ways that I rely on myself: ways that will lead me to destruction if I do not submit them to you.

Please don't leave me in this state of independence. I want my heart to be subject to you in all ways and in all areas. By your Spirit, give me humility to rely upon you and faith to lean into you. I know that my pride is abhorrent to you, God. I pray that you would forgive me, and I would remain your humble servant.

Father, you are my refuge and peace. I know that I can come to you and find solace when I am overcome by the world. You are my rock and my fortress. You are my hope: a towering beacon in the stormy sea.

Be Still

"Be still, and know that I am God.
I will be exalted among the nations,
I will be exalted in the earth!"

PSALM 46:10 ESV

Sometimes I love to do something new: choose a different path, forge ahead, and explore a new way. This can get me into trouble, and my curiosity can entangle me in things I dared not do. Fail me not, Father, in guiding my path. Lead me over safe ground and beside steady waters.

When I am thirsty and hungry, whether in flesh or in spirit, please take care of me. Show me your glory and the power that you hold in my life. It is you my soul needs, and I don't want to forget it.

God, I can come to you at all times. You won't hold back from me because you are compassionate and good to all. It is your desire that all men know you and choose life. I have life because I know you and believe in you.

For Ever and Ever

This God is our God for ever and ever;
he will be our guide even to the end.

PSALM 48:14 NIV

My road is long, and I am far from home. I have traveled many places, and there has been nowhere to settle down. My spirit is restless and anxious to find the right spot—a home where peace and contentment reside. In my heart and my mind, I know this is found in you alone, God. Somehow, you must help me to get there despite myself.

I feel like the weary traveler who drags his feet just to make it a few steps. My journey overwhelms me at times, and I need you to encourage me. Be my home away from home, a resting place to lay my head. Be my comfort, Holy Spirit.

God, you are my peace. Though my path is filled with trouble, and I carry burdens too much to bear, I can make it because you are with me. Your burdens are easy, and your yoke is light. You call me your son. I can walk, perhaps even skip, with a confidence that I will get home to you.

Never Forgotten

"How could a loving mother forget her nursing child and
not deeply love the one she bore?
Even if a there is a mother who forgets her child,
I could never, no never, forget you."

ISAIAH 49:15 TPT

Father, I find comfort in your words of compassion for
me. I know the love of a parent for their child. It is such a
strong bond that we all experience whether as a parent or
a child. You created this love, and it is driven by sacrifice
and commitment. It is poured out freely to me, and I want
to embrace it and live by it.

You know the struggle in my heart to accept myself and
love me for how you made me. Help me to be more in tune
with your Spirit, to recognize your grace over me, and to
trust the work that you are completing in me.

*You are faithful, and your love endures forever. You are not
distant from me, God. You walk with me in my troubles,
and you stand with me in my fight. I know that my success
is rooted in your presence flowing through me. Thank you
for never leaving nor forsaking me.*

Engraved

"See, I have engraved you on the palms of my hands;
your walls are ever before me."

ISAIAH 49:16 NIV

Lord, I know that you hold me closer than I comprehend. In my heart I often think I am walking this life alone. I do trust that you are with me, but I feel alone. Help me to sense your presence with me, to be filled with your Spirit anew each day.

I want my life to be written in your book, my name written on your hands. I ask that you would help me to reach the potential that you have for me. I want my life to mean something to you.

You have kept me for yourself. You gave your life for me, Jesus. Because of your sacrifice and your willingness to suffer, I have been redeemed. I am yours. I trust that you will lead and guide me in your ways. I believe that you are for me and not against me. Your peace will abide in me because my mind is set on you.

Made Steadfast

The God of all grace, who called you to his eternal glory
in Christ, after you have suffered a little while,
will himself restore you and make you strong,
firm and steadfast.

1 PETER 5:10 NIV

Jesus, I know this life does not promise glory and peace.
You said I will face trouble and I know I am suffering the
consequences of sin and death ruling this age. I long for
you to come back and make all things right. I want my
heart to be strong, believing in your ability to help me
endure.

You know the things I am going through, and I pray that
you would give me your peace and joy in the midst of my
pain. Give me a greater faith, Lord. Help me in my unbelief.

*God, you are gracious and kind. You power is demonstrated
in my weakness, and I accept that I am a broken vessel
upheld by your hand. You will be glorified in me. I trust that
you will make me steadfast in you.*

My Justification

"Blessed are those who are persecuted
for righteousness' sake,
For theirs is the kingdom of heaven."

MATTHEW 5:10 NKJV

It is within me to admit my fault and rely upon the only one who can save me to do so. I confess my sin and admit my mistakes before you, God. You are my Lord, and I ask that your forgiveness and righteousness would be my covering.

Jesus, when I am judged, I only have you as my justification to stand before the Father. Please continue to help me walk humbly before you and accept what you have done for me as enough. You know that I want to please you, to do things that maybe would make it appear that I am good. I am not. I need you, Jesus.

You alone are holy and righteous. All of your judgments are just. I deserved punishment and death, but you redeemed me by your grace and called me as your own. Thank you, Jesus! I am so grateful for your redemption and the promises you have for me.

Shield of Love

You bless the godly, O Lord;
you surround them with your shield of love.

PSALM 5:12 NIV

Father, I want you to see me as godly. How do I do this when I know the wickedness in my own heart? I pray that you would break through the darkness that clouds my mind. Let your Word penetrate my heart and show me the name that you call me by.

Help me to see what you have done in me, to transform me into the likeness of your Son, Jesus. You are at work in me despite my own troubles. I want to believe in what you are doing in me, that I would see how you are my shield and my Savior.

Thank you for your great work, Jesus. You have given me your Spirit and called me by a new name. I am no longer a slave to sin, but I am your son. I am redeemed, holy, Christlike, and set on a path for resurrection. You do such great work!

Approach with Joy

"This is the confidence we have in approaching God:
that if we ask anything according to his will,
he hears us."

JOHN 5:14 NIV

Hear my cry, God. Attend unto my prayer. From the ends of the earth, I cry to you. Lead me to the rock that is higher than I. I need you to be my strong tower and a shield about me. Prolong my life and let me live in peace. Give me your mercy and truth that my heart and mind would be protected.

Help me to know confidence before you. That when I ask you will answer, and that when I call, you will come to me. Father, I approach you humbly, knowing that my very existence is in your hands.

Father, you give me life and sustain me. I can come to you in joy and anticipation of your acceptance and love. You hear me even when I feel I am far from you; you draw near to me. Thank you for your goodness toward me. I find that my heart is softened by your kindness. You bring me to pleasant places. I can trust in you.

Do Good

Trust the Lord and do good.
Live in the land and feed on truth.
Enjoy serving the Lord
and he will give you what you want.
Depend on the Lord;
trust him, and he will take care of you.

PSALM 37:3-5 NCV

Lord, my prayer has been that my heart's desires would match yours. I know that when I walk in this manner, the things I want are the things you desire. Help me to delight in you and take pleasure in discovering who you are and what you are doing on the earth.

I want creativity and adventure to be driven by you. Help me to trust in you and to do good in the land. Give me eyes to see past those who are wicked and seem to prevail. I don't want to become weary of doing good because I know at the right time, I will reap what I have sown.

Father, I know that I can trust in you because of your goodness and character. Your love is eternal and enduring. Your compassion never fails. You are love and justice perfectly combined. I am able to walk confidently before you not because of who I am but because of who you are.

Honoring Parents

"Honor your father and your mother, as the LORD your God has commanded you, that your days may be long, and that it may be well with you in the land which the LORD your God is giving you."

DEUTERONOMY 5:16 NKJV

Father, thank you for my parents. Perhaps I did not always recognize it, but they are worthy of my gratitude. I am here because of them and you. Give them knowledge of you and a desire to seek you. Pour out upon them your grace and mercy, that their lives would reflect you to others.

Strengthen them in their later years and help them know your closeness. I pray that you would bless them as they have blessed me. Beyond what they have given, give to them. I ask for your peace to be upon them.

God, you are the best Father. You know exactly what I need, and you give me all that you have. My inheritance in you is unfading and will not perish. It remains in wait for me. I love that I have this promise to look forward to. But greater than this is the blessing of being with you for eternity; I am excited to be with the one who loves me most.

Called to Pray

Confess your sins to each other and pray for each other so that you may be healed. The prayer of a righteous person is powerful and effective.

JAMES 5:16 NIV

Jesus, you know me. You have called me to seek you and pray. I ask for your help to pray because I do not truly know how. I also ask that you would help me to be vulnerable with my close friends. I know you want me to be open and humble.

You don't want me to be independent of you or of the body of believers you have given me. Help me to trust in you and share myself with those around me. I know that love is a sacrifice, humility is weakness, and caring is the work of a servant. You call me to these, and it is so hard to do. Help me.

Jesus, you have made me righteous by your sacrifice on the cross. Therefore, every prayer I pray in faith is powerful and effective. I believe in you, your justification of me, and my status through you. I know that my faith is what allows me to live and walk with you. You equip me for every good work. Help me to be humble, loving, and caring.

Walk Rightly

I will give you a new heart, and a new spirit I will put within you. And I will remove the heart of stone from your flesh and give you a heart of flesh.

EZEKIEL 36:26 ESV

I have died with Christ, and it is no longer I who live, but Christ lives in me. Let that statement be my mantra. God, I want to know this in my heart, that I would be passionate about it and identify myself by it.

Help me to be certain of my place in you. Give me your strength of purpose and mind. Pour out your Spirit on me, so I walk in your statutes and prove your purposes to be good. I need you, God. I love that you call me. Help me to hear your voice and answer you.

God, I am a new creation. I no longer am obedient to sin and death but am free to love you and follow you. In you I have all that I need to live a victorious life. You have given me joy, peace, love, and self-control. You have given me many more things to walk rightly before you.

Called to You

Anyone who belongs to Christ
has become a new person.
The old life is gone;
a new life has begun!

2 CORINTHIANS 5:17 NLT

Jesus, I am pleased that you called me to yourself. I continue to ask that you would help me to call on your name. Have mercy on me. I pray again, Lord Jesus Christ, have mercy on me! I want to be a passionate follower of your ways and your desires.

I know that when I take enjoyment in you, I will find what my heart searches for. Pour into me your Spirit so I can know the deeper things of you. Holy Spirit, show me the truth and the life that I have because I am in Christ.

Jesus, it is by your blood that I am redeemed. You have called me out of darkness into your light. You have called me chosen, a holy man because of your work on the cross. I am saved and changed by the work of your Spirit within me. I submit to you.

As Far as Possible

God has made all things new,
and reconciled us to himself,
and given us the ministry
of reconciling others to God.

2 Corinthians 5:18 TPT

I want reconciliation to flow throughout the body of Christ. Jesus, help it to start with me. Give me boldness to speak out against my fears and the concern of being hurt. Take my offense and hardness of heart away and soften me. I pray that no offense would be held in my heart.

As a dead man, I resign myself to making peace with all men as far as it is possible. You are my portion and my cup; give me eyes for you and you alone. Help my trust in you to exceed my thoughts and my concerns.

God, you are the great creator. You made everything I see by speaking a word. I have no doubt in your ability to make all things new. I trust in you to change me and mold me into Christ. By your Spirit I am being sanctified and renewed. You are preparing me for the day of your return.

Extravagant Love

Continue to walk surrendered to the extravagant love of Christ, for he surrendered his life as a sacrifice for us. His great love for us was pleasing to God, like an aroma of adoration—a sweet healing fragrance.

EPHESIANS 5:2 TPT

I want to surrender myself to you, but I am struggling, Father. It is hard not be self-reliant even in my close relationships. It is even harder with you, who I can't physically touch. I know you say how great it is for me to believe without having seen you, and this is true, I have not seen you. Because of this, it can be easy to forget. To not keep you in the forefront of all I do.

Help me. I need to feel you close to me. I want to understand your presence beyond just the physical. We are both spiritual beings, but I can't wait to physically be present with you.

You surrendered all for me and give me the strength to do the same, Jesus. Continue to pour out your Spirit so I am equipped with all I need to bear good fruit.

The Fruit

The Holy Spirit produces this kind of fruit in our lives:
love, joy, peace, patience, kindness,
goodness, faithfulness.

GALATIANS 5:22 NLT

Spirit of God, give me these good things so my life is pleasing to you. I know that if I can walk in these, I will be a content man. What is better than a man who has everything he needs because he wants what he has? I know if you can fill me with the fruit of your Spirit, I will be this man.

Help me to overcome my own demons: the things that plague me and keep me from drawing close to you. Overwhelm me with your goodness and give me a strength that is only found in you.

Holy Spirit, thank you for dwelling with me. You are in my life every day, and you draw me closer to Jesus. I know that I have all that I need to obey your voice and live a content life. Continue to fill me with your purposes and passion. You show me the way to the Father, and I submit my heart to you.

Every Morning

LORD, every morning you hear my voice.
Every morning, I tell you what I need,
and I wait for your answer.

PSALM 5:3 NCV

God, this is kind of true of me. I do speak with you often even if it is short. I want to speak with you more and I want to hear your voice. Help me to wait for your answer. Give me an attentive heart that is able to patiently wait.

I am like a candle in the wind, easily blown out. Please be a shield about me to keep my flame alight. When I miss time with you, gently remind me to seek you out. Draw me by your Spirit to keep pursuing you. I know my propensity to pursue instant gratification in simple things; steer me away from this and give me a heart devoted to you.

How great that you listen to me. Thank you, Father, for caring enough that you hear my prayers. Thank you for being faithful to answer me. You are the reason I can get up tomorrow and keep on keeping on! Thank you for your strength today.

Growth in Adversity

We glory in our sufferings, because we know that
suffering produces perseverance; perseverance
character; and character, hope.

ROMANS 5:3-4 NIV

I grow most when I face adversity and do not run from it.
Help me, Jesus, to know perseverance in the face of my
troubles. I do not have a problem facing difficulty, but I do
need your endurance. Also, when I do feel overwhelmed,
I ask that you would first protect me, and then help me to
find others to support me.

I know I don't face adversity alone and that you have
placed around me an effective community of support. I
ask that you would remind me to be vulnerable with them
when the time comes.

*God, your promises are true, and I know that you will help
me make it to the finish line. I may be weary and tired,
but you will give me strength. When I am hard pressed, I
know that you stop me from being crushed. When I am in
despair, you do not abandon me. You are with me always
and your commitment to me is legitimate.*

You Will Comfort

"Blessed are those who mourn,
for they shall be comforted."

MATTHEW 5:4 ESV

You are my comfort, Holy Spirit. You were sent to love me with compassion and care. Please speak the truth to me and help me endure what lays ahead. I know the truth of the world I live in, that it is in fast decay and that men are full of wickedness. This I know will not relent.

In light of this, I ask that you would give me endurance and a plan for how to overcome. I am saddened by the state of this world, and I know it grieves you more. You will come back and make this right, and you will comfort your people.

Jesus, judge of men's intentions, you destroy the works of the wicked and remove them from around me. You have authority to deal with the enemy, and I praise you for your good works. It is of great comfort to me that you are the judge and executioner. You are full of mercy, kindness, and understanding, but you will not put up with rebellion either.

Fruit of Fullness

This is no empty hope, for God himself is the one who has prepared us for this wonderful destiny. And to confirm this promise, he has given us the Holy Spirit, like an engagement ring, as a guarantee.

2 Corinthians 5:5 tpt

Holy Spirit, thank you for dwelling in me. Fill me with hope and promise. I want to be an overcomer. I want to know the praises of my God every day. I ask that from my mouth and by my actions men would know the blessing that it is to follow you.

Continue to help me tolerate the broken society around me, to speak the truth in love, and bring me to the knowledge of you. I need the fullness of your Spirit, the fruit that he brings, to live this life and to successfully find myself awaiting your return.

Holy Spirit, thank you for not passing me by. You are preparing me and making me ready for Christ's return. Thank you for working with me on my sanctification, for filling me with love, joy, peace, forbearance, kindness, goodness, faithfulness, gentleness, and self-control.

Cutting Edge

"Blessed are the gentle,
for they shall inherit the earth."

MATTHEW 5:5 NASB

I want to receive my inheritance from you, God. Help me
not to look to the things of this earth whether possessions
or people. Fill me with anticipation for what you have
for me. No eye has seen, nor ear heard, no mind has
conceived, what you have in store for me as I continue to
love and pursue you.

Give me that cutting edge so I can last through all the
difficulty I will face and be ready at your return. Help me
to be gentle in my speech with others and to love them as
you love me. I want to be as compassionate and gracious
as you are, so I may inherit all you have for me.

*I love your diverse nature, God. You are so gentle, kind,
and compassionate, yet you are just, strong, and bold. You
speak the truth and know what every man needs to hear.
Your Spirit is speaking to me consistently about my life and
the way I should walk. You are even gentle in the way you
guide me. Thank you.*

No Shame

Hope does not put us to shame, because God's love has been poured into our hearts through the Holy Spirit who has been given to us.

ROMANS 5:5 ESV

Why do the wicked prevail? How is it that your people God, are seemingly trampled underfoot by those who run to do evil? There are so many hurt souls, yet you call us to hope in you. How do I do this when I see such atrocities?

Fill me again with your promises and lift my eyes to you, the Savior of my life. Bring to mind all your promises and the justice that you will one day bring to the earth. Fill me with your love and the Spirit who teaches me truth. Allow me to survive this wicked world without shame.

There will be a day when all shame is taken away and your justice reigns with your love. You will make things right, Jesus. We can trust in your leadership and the direction of our lives. We know your power and your authority will prevail. Come, King Jesus!

Bow Low

If you bow low in God's awesome presence,
he will eventually exalt you
as you leave the timing in his hands.

1 Peter 5:6 tpt

God, you know my impatience to see things happen. I
naturally want to push for things when I want them. You
know how I am, and I ask for self-control and patience.
You have a plan and I want to trust in it, but sometimes my
actions fail my heart's desire.

Although I want to do good and I delight in your law, I
see another law at work in me waging war and making
me a prisoner of sin. Thank you for the freedom I have in
Christ! Help me to continue to bravely follow after you and
embrace the work of your Spirit in me.

*I am bowed down before you, God. You are awesome, and
in my reverence for you, I sing out with praises. You are
worthy of glory and honor. There is none who is like you. I
thank you that in my humility you are the lifter of my head,
and you cover my shame. I am safe in you.*

First Pursuit

"Blessed are those who hunger and thirst for righteousness, for they will be filled."

MATTHEW 5:6 NRSV

Lord, your Word is good for me. Help me to eat and be filled. Speak to me in the night watches and lead me in the daytime. Show me how you have made me righteous and have set me apart for yourself.

I want to know the contentment of walking rightly before you above any other passion. Show me how to make you my number one pursuit. Above all things I want to chase after righteousness: to run to you, my justification. I want to be blessed by you.

Those who seek you will find you, God. You are the rewarder of the diligent. There is great blessing in reading your Word and spending time on my knees before you. Thank you that you fulfill me and allow me to walk with you. I will throw away all other passions for this one thing: to glorify you and enjoy you forever.

Tender Care

Pour out all your worries and stress upon him and leave
them there, for he always tenderly cares for you.

1 PETER 5:7 TPT

God, I want to know how you handle all the cares of the
world at once. It helps me to be comforted understanding
how big you are. I know what it means to care for others,
whether as a spouse, parent, or a friend. It is hard not to
be overwhelmed by what others are going through when
there is nothing I can do. Yet, you want to take all my cares
and those of the world? How great you are, God!

What I would like to see in my life is a more consistent
response to facing adversity. I would like my first thought
to be that I need you. Father, I want to call out to you right
away.

*What God is there like you? No one else takes away my sin,
forgives me, sets me on a righteous path, and encourages
me to give them my worry and concerns. You are the best
father anyone could ever want. I give you my worries and
anxieties. I trust that you will tenderly take care of me.*

Only Reprieve

"Blessed are the merciful,
for they shall receive mercy."

MATTHEW 5:7 NASB

Merciful Savior, I cry out to you alone. There is no reprieve for me in any other person. I ask that you would take my sins and my brokenness and forgive me. Help me to show the same mercy to others that you extend to me.

I want to trust in you enough that I do not take offense at others' pain. I know we are all broken, and sometimes I take another person's damage upon myself. I ask that you would show me the love you have for others so when someone is being unintentionally hurtful, I would reflect the way you feel.

Father, you are so kind to me. You know that I am not as merciful as you are, yet you are still so kind. You have given me your Spirit and the ability to love well. Thank you for helping me to be like you are. Thank you for the blessing of mercy.

Slow Process

I know that you will welcome me into your house,
for I am covered by your covenant of mercy and love.
So I come to your sanctuary with deepest awe
to bow in worship and adore you.

PSALM 5:7 TPT

Lord, you are so good! I do worship you, Father. I need your love and mercy. Help me to see my own brokenness so I become more dependent on you. You call me to come and be with you, and sometimes I resist. I am sorry for this.

I pray that you would assist me in the slow process of surrendering my heart and my will to you. I often feel like my heart is there, but I fight you with what I want to do. Shadow me, God, wherever I am walking, and lead me in the way you want me to go.

Thank you for your welcome, Jesus. I love that I can wake up each morning and you are there, waiting for me to acknowledge you. What God is there like this? There is no pretense with you. You are simply good all the time.

Your Beloved

Christ proved God's passionate love for us by dying in our place while we were still lost and ungodly!

ROMANS 5:8 TPT

Oh Lord, you know me. I am so grateful that you have seen Christ and not me! When I consider your ways and the work of your hands, I am humbled. Why are you even mindful of me, considering what you can do and what you can make? Yet I am part of your beloved.

I have within me the Spirit of him who was raised from the dead. I want you to help me walk like it; straighten my paths, Lord Jesus. Continue to fill me with your Spirit. I ask that you would convict me of sin, righteousness, and judgment. Prepare my heart for your return.

Father, you alone are God. You have all authority over the enemy, and I trust in your power, judgments, and love. You are magnified above all other gods. There is none who stands out like you, my Savior and my King!

NOVEMBER

Be faithful to pray as
intercessors who are fully alert
and giving thanks to God.

COLOSSIANS 4:2 TPT

Truth and Light

Once you were full of darkness,
but now you have light from the Lord.
So live as people of light!
For this light within you produces
only what is good and right and true.

EPHESIANS 5:8-9 NLT

Father, show me your ways. Fill me with your truth and light. I know that in my heart, without you, there is a darkness I cannot escape. But because of you, I can walk in what is right. I want to know more of your ways and embrace them as my own.

Holy Spirit, help me to know you more and to hear your voice. I want to do what is good and right. I pray that my life would be pleasing to you, Lord.

You are my light and my life. My salvation comes from you alone. There is no other god but you, God! You are the perfect example of how I can live and walk this life. Jesus, all that I need is discovered in you and because of this I can trust in your leadership. You have placed within me your Spirit of truth and he teaches me your ways.

Hidden in You

The Lord God helps me,
Therefore, I am not disgraced;
Therefore, I have set my face like flint,
And I know that I will not be ashamed.

Isaiah 50:7 nasb

I look to you, Lord. It is when my face is lifted to you that I can live my life successfully. I pray that my mind would remain open to your Word, and my heart would be tender to your Holy Spirit.

When I am overwhelmed with my sin and I feel like my bones are rotting, come and save me from myself. Wash me clean and restore me so I am not ashamed. There are those around me who want to see me fail, but I am hidden in you, and I pray that you would be a shield about me.

Lord God, you are my helper. You are my protection in the storms of life. I can come to you and not fear. You are my shield and my salvation. Continue to show me your ways and guide me in your truth. I trust in you.

Far from Perfect

Have mercy on me, O God,
because of your unfailing love.
Because of your great compassion,
blot out the stain of my sins.

PSALM 51:1 NLT .

I know that I need mercy. I need it from you, God, and from people. I am far from perfect. I know that is ok with you, Jesus, because you are kind and gracious. Help me to make people feel that way too, that when I see their imperfection and brokenness, I would make them feel unashamed.

Help me to love people like you do, showing compassion and kindness. Holy Spirit I pray that your fruit would be evident in my life. Thank you for forgiving me and cleansing me of my sin.

I am saved by you, Jesus. You have forgiven me and have made me clean. I am so grateful for your salvation. I look forward to the resurrection I will experience in you. I will be a new man, made like you, completely free and full of glory!

Tender Heart

My sacrifice, O God, is a broken spirit;
a broken and contrite heart you,
God, will not despise.

PSALM 51:17 NIV

I want a heart that is tender to you, Holy Spirit. Help me to be sensitive to you and your ways. Show me the truth of my life and help me not to hide behind any false realities.

I want to be genuine with you and with others. I want my life to represent you well. I know that humility is highly valuable, and you will support me when I embrace it. I bow down before you, God. I admit that without you, my life is worthless. I want my life to glorify you.

Father, thank you for sending your Son to die for me. Jesus, I praise you for your sacrifice and for saving me. Thank you for sending the Holy Spirit to me so I can walk in the truth, I can love well, and I can be comforted in this troubled life. Thank you for dwelling with me every day and teaching me your ways.

Not Worthy

He was pierced for our rebellion, crushed for our sins.
He was beaten so we could be whole.
He was whipped so we could be healed.

Isaiah 53:5 NLT

Jesus, I cry out to you, cleanse me from my sins and make me righteous as you are. Help me to walk in your ways and love you as you loved me. It is hard to read this verse and to think about the suffering you incurred for my sake. I am not worthy of a King, the Creator, humbling himself as you did and then suffering and dying for me.

I am completely humbled by what you have done to save all of your creation. Thank you. You have done so much for me, and I pray that somehow I can do something in return. Take my little effort and make it large in your kingdom.

You are so good, Lord. You gave up all of yourself and your position to become something you created. Wow, Jesus, you are so loving, humble, and kind. Though I pale in comparison, you continue to love me. You pour out your blessing on me and speak words of kindness over me. Thank you for your salvation!

I Surrender

Give your burdens to the LORD,
and he will take care of you.
He will not permit the godly to slip and fall.

PSALM 55:22 NLT

Lord, you know me and my ways. Help me to do what is right and choose the hard things. I tend to find the easy way and wander away. Bring my heart back to you. Woo me to yourself and help me to walk in trepidation of your judgments.

Show me my brokenness and may it cause humility in my heart. Then I will walk in godliness, and you will carry my burdens. I pray that you would take care of me, Jesus. You know so much more about me than I understand myself. Heal my heart and make me a better lover of you and of people.

You are so kind, Father, to choose to carry my burdens. You have already given so much to me and I am forever grateful. You shower me with kindness, take away my sins, and make my journey pleasant. What a great God I serve! You will make me obedient to you. I surrender.

It Is Right

"As the heavens are higher than the earth,
so are My ways higher than your ways,
and My thoughts than your thoughts."

ISAIAH 55:9 NKJV

I pray that the words of my mouth and the mediations of my heart will be pleasing to you, God. We are so different in so many ways, yet you choose to be with me, and for this I am thankful. I want to think as you do, and then to act based upon sound knowledge and understanding.

Help me to know your ways and your thoughts. You have given me your Spirit who guides me. I want to be a better listener. I want to be encouraged to seek you first in all things even when I don't feel like it—because I know it is right.

God, you are mighty, and your ways are perfect. No one could script what you do any better than you have done it. You have given men freedom to choose, and fail, and be redeemed. You have saved me. You let me choose what I did, and I chose you. I continue to choose you because I trust in you.

Choose Again

In the day that I'm afraid,
I lay all my fears before you
and trust in you with all my heart.

PSALM 56:3 TPT

Yes, Jesus! I choose you again. You know the fears that grip my heart and the triggers that make me respond with strong emotion. I lay these before you. Help me to trust that you are in them. Guide me, Holy Spirit, in the truths that Jesus has for me. Show me the ways that I can grow in the knowledge of you and the mystery of your will.

Make me holy and blameless in you and continue to lavish upon me your wisdom and insight. I want to lean upon you and let the world know that it is ok for me to do so. Help me to be bold about my weakness.

God, I can rely upon you. You are closer to me than a brother, more comforting than a mother, and wiser than my father. I can trust in you because of who you are: honest, caring, loving, kind, strong, and able. Who is there like this, perfect in all their ways? God, you are perfect, and this is what I need.

Reflection of You

Your love is so extravagant it reaches to the heavens,
Your faithfulness so astonishing it stretches to the sky!

PSALM 57:10 TPT

You amaze me, God. When I ponder your ways, your interaction with your creation, and your continued care for it, I am so thankful that I know you. I pray that you would help me to wake each day reminded of your greatness.

Give me your eyes for your creation. Help me to love all with a love like yours. Develop my heart to demonstrate the same character you have to others. I want to be faithful to you as you are to me. When people see me, I hope they see some of you.

I am so tiny in a vast world, with a great God, yet you look upon me and smile. How great it is to know you and be known by you. Your love amazes me. You care about the smallest of things like they mean so much to you. What an astounding, praiseworthy, awesome God you are.

Full of Worship

I will sing of Your power;
Yes, I will sing aloud of Your mercy in the morning;
For You have been my defense
And refuge in the day of my trouble.

PSALM 59:16 NKJV

I want my heart to be filled with worship. I know that those who are full of gratitude and praise are people of positive attitude who have good days. I enjoy the good days. Even when things are failing around me, I wake up winning when I can keep my mind on you.

Help me Jesus, to see you at work despite the wickedness of the world. It is overwhelming to ponder the darkness that surrounds me, yet your love shatters it and covers me. Help me to hide my heart in your bunker of love.

I know that I can rest in you, because you care for me, God. You said I can bring my anxieties to you because you care for me. This is true and I find peace in you because you take away my worries. You show me the promises you have given and have kept. I can trust in you because you are faithful and true.

An Actuality

God is not unjust; he will not overlook your work and the love that you showed for his sake in serving the saints, as you still do.

HEBREWS 6:10 NRSV

Lord, help me to love those around me. Show me how to serve others as you did. You were so good at loving others and speaking into their lives what they needed to hear. You showed them the ways of your Father. I want to do the same for those I am with.

I pray that as I live and speak, they would see your life represented in mine. Give me your sacrificial love that lays itself down for the benefit of others. I know you see my heart and you are pleased with my desire. Thankfully, you have grace for my failings. Help make my desire to please you an actuality.

I love your justice, God. Though I don't see it all yet, it will come to fruition. You will come back and make all things right one day. I thank you that I am able to throw myself at your mercy and you lift me up and forgive me. You have saved me from your judgments!

Master of Grace

Sin shall no longer be your master,
because you are not under the law,
but under grace.

ROMANS 6:14 NIV

I submit my heart to you, Jesus. I want you to be my master. I want the Holy Spirit to direct my life. I want your words to be written on my heart, that you would be my God, and I would be a part of your people. Help me surrender myself on a daily basis. It is not an easy task when I am trying to fight my carnal desires.

Holy Spirit, give me your strength and comfort. I want to be able to walk like Jesus: able to suffer and do God's will because I fully trust in you. Help me not to look to other men to make things ok. I want to look to you alone.

Thank you for being merciful to me, God. I love your kindness and your delight in me. I know that my humility before you is pleasing. You are the lover of the lowly and lifter of the broken. You give me endurance and hope. I trust in you.

My Life and Truth

Teach those who are rich in this world not to be proud and not to trust in their money, which is so unreliable. Their trust should be in God, who richly gives us all we need for our enjoyment.

1 TIMOTHY 6:17 NLT

Lord, I don't want a heart that is caught up in chasing the things of this world. I want my life to be seen as one which wholeheartedly pursues you. Help me because I know how far I am from this reality. All that the world offers me is unreliable, a short-term replacement for you, and it leads to death.

You are my life and my truth, and I seek you. I pray that you would help me by changing my heart to be passionate for the things of you and dead to the pleasures of this life. Your pleasures are so much better!

You delight in giving to us, God. You do not hold back your goodness from me. You do want me to seek it out, and I will find it! I know that the joy I have in you is better, longer lasting, and more intense than anything I can find in this life. Continue to fill me with your Spirit and the delight that I seek and find in you.

Loving Truth

It is impossible for God to lie for we know that his
promise and his vow will never change! And now
we have run into his heart to hide ourselves in his
faithfulness. This is where we find his strength and
comfort, for he empowers us to seize what has already
been established ahead of time—an unshakeable hope.

HEBREWS 6:18 TPT

I love your truth and I want it to fill my heart. I can
understand myself better when I know your Word and
the Spirit opens my eyes to it. Give me a heart that
comprehends you, God. I want to know you better and love
your ways above my own. You have such great things to
show me, but I quickly get caught up in the worries and
concerns of this life.

On top of these, I have quick fixes that make me feel
better. Some besetting sins hold me back. It is frustrating,
but I pray that you will continue to mature me into the man
you called me to be.

*I run to you in response to you running to me. I know it's
not one sided. You love me more than I love you. You are
so good, God! You are faithful, patient, enduring, kind, and
merciful. I trust in your great character.*

Hope as an Anchor

We have this hope as an anchor for the soul,
firm and secure.

HEBREWS 6:19 NIV

Hope is helpful to me, Father. It comes from the truth of your promises. Because you cannot lie, and your words never return to you void, I know they are working in me.

When I am struggling with the gloom of this life—when I see the weak being harmed and the injustices of bad men succeeding—I really need your promises. When I am troubled by my own sin, or suffering from selfish introspection, I need your hope. I pray that you would remind me of your promises and fill me with the hope that gives me endurance and joy.

I only have hope because of your good character, Jesus. I know that the words you speak will come true. Otherwise, my life would be aimless and end in death. But you have rescued me, set me upon a firm foundation, and my life now is secure in you. Thank you for the great inheritance I have in you, the richness of your glory, and life with you forever.

The Blessing

The LORD bless you and keep you;
the LORD make his face to shine upon you,
and be gracious to you;
the LORD lift up his countenance upon you,
and give you peace.

NUMBERS 6:24-26 NRSV

I reflect on the many times I have had this prayed over me, prayed it over someone, or listened to it prayed over others. It is a prayer spoken across the planet over your people, God, and I ask that you would fulfill it in us all.

Lord, please guard my way. Keep me on your paths of righteousness and bless my steps. May your eyes of favor be upon me in all that I do, that your grace would be prevalent in my life. Give me your peace and fill me with your presence, that your countenance and your joy would be mine.

Father, you love me. You care about me. Your delight is in me. What have I done to merit this favor? Nothing except being a child you chose for yourself. I choose you too. I delight in you. Thank you for your grace and mercy.

Secure in You

"Look at the birds. They don't plant or harvest or store food in barns, for your heavenly Father feeds them. And aren't you far more valuable to him than they are? Can all your worries add a single moment to your life?"

MATTHEW 6:26 NLT

I love your creation, Lord. It reminds me of how amazing you are. It should also remind me of how much you care about my life. I forget this at times. Jesus, remind my soul of this. Make it secure in me so I can trust in you alone.

When I see the birds feeding, and the grass growing, remind me of your care for me. Even more so, when my heart is swamped with the worries of this life and I am wading through the mire of a wicked world, give me your peace. Show me how much you care and love me, so I am not overwhelmed.

I can trust in your care for me. You know my path, God. You speak life into every situation I face. There is nothing that can separate us. Nothing can come between you and me and our love for each other. I am secure in you.

Content and Satisfied

"Seek the Kingdom of God above all else, and live righteously, and he will give you everything you need."

MATTHEW 6:33 NLT

Lord, you are my righteousness. I know that my life without you will not end in anything but vanity and worthlessness. My end without you is non-existence: a lonely and sad existence. I want you to fill my heart and show me my value in you.

I believe in you, and I want my life to be a meaningful expression of you to others. Help me to look to you alone for my needs and take joy in your Spirit. Fill me, Holy Spirit, with your passion and drive. I want to seek you with great intention.

You are my provider, Father. I can look to you and be satisfied. In you I am content. I trust in your provision and your guidance. You light my way and speak truth over me. I can lean upon you because you are faithful. I am so pleased that you are my God.

Joy of Salvation

"All that the Father gives me will come to me,
and whoever comes to me I will never cast out."

JOHN 6:37 ESV

Jesus, I come to you! I needed a Savior, and you saved me. Holy Spirit continue to fulfill in me the great purposes of God, that I would be testimony to your greatness. Be merciful to me. I need it from you because I know my weakness and failings.

I see my sin and my broken humanity. I compare this to a perfect and righteous God. How can I even live apart from your great kindness? I am thankful and humbled by you, God. I pray for the joy of your salvation to shine through me to others.

Your faithfulness is enduring. Your love knows no bounds. You are my joy and my salvation. Because you are great, I need nothing. Your character and your promises are true. I trust in you because you are good.

Judge Not

"Judge not, and you will not be judged;
condemn not, and you will not be condemned;
forgive, and you will be forgiven."

LUKE 6:37 ESV

Lord, forgive me for my judgments of others. Fill me with
your compassion and kindness. Give me understanding for
others and insight to help them in their need. You know
how much I need, and the weaknesses I have. Yet, you love
and care for me.

I throw myself at your mercy, Jesus Christ. Help me to be
merciful to others. Holy Spirit, you are my helper, and you
are with me to give me fruit that is good. Continue to work
in me so the harvest is plentiful and righteous.

*Jesus, you are a wise judge. When all men stand before
you, you know how to separate the sheep from the goats.
You are a good judge. You shower me with mercy and
kindness, and you help me to do this for others. Thank you,
Holy Spirit, for bearing good fruit in me.*

Giving Generously

"Give, and you will receive. You will be given much.
Pressed down, shaken together, and running over,
it will spill into your lap. The way you give to others
is the way God will give to you."

LUKE 6:38 NCV

Sometimes I am caught up in my own story, so much so that I cannot tend to others as I should. Holy Spirit, shake me out of my apathy and self-centeredness. You promise to take care of me when I trust in you and cast aside my worries.

Help me to give lavishly of myself and demonstrate the care you have for me to others. I can see what you want to do in me, and how I could be of great help to others, but I also have to figure out the balance of giving and receiving. I know if I am not taking time to be with you and receive, I will get burned out. Guide me, Jesus.

God, you bless me with your presence. It pours out through me to others. Your joy, your peace, and your love give me all I need to reflect you to others. I can throw myself into you because you are trustworthy.

A Good Reward

Remember that the Lord will reward
each one of us for the good we do.

EPHESIANS 6:8 NLT

Lord, it is good to understand that when I am successful
at obeying you, there will be a reward. You are not blind
to my intentions which means you see me and know
my heart. That feels good and bad. Good because I am
confident that I want to do right by you, but also that you
see the snippets of wickedness still in me.

Blot out my sin, God, and continue to sanctify me by
the work of your Spirit. Let me bear good fruit for your
kingdom and extend your glory throughout the earth.

*You are good and a rewarder of those who diligently seek
you. God, your rich grace is poured out upon me, and you
continue to fill me with the knowledge of your will in all
spiritual wisdom and understanding. It is you who works
your good will in me for your pleasure. Because of this, I
will share in the inheritance of the saints.*

Already Known

"Your Father already knows what you need before you ask him."

MATTHEW 6:8 TPT

Father, thank you for hearing my prayer. Enlarge my tent and push back the enemy from around me. Encapsulate me in your love and protect me from those who wish to bring me harm. Remove wickedness from my heart and fill me with your truth.

Show me your way, Jesus, and help me to depend upon your Spirit today. Fill my mind with the knowledge of your will and help me to surrender my way to you. Continue to grant me life and forgive me for my wrongdoing. I am delighted to serve you.

You are so good, God. I don't even need to ask you for what I must have because you have already provided it. I walk in faith that you are my provider and the good shepherd who leads me on paths of righteousness. You are awake, watching over me when I am sleeping and protecting me. I love you being in my life.

Harvest of Blessing

Let's not get tired of doing what is good.
At just the right time we will reap a harvest of blessing
if we don't give up.

GALATIANS 6:9 NLT

Give me your endurance, Lord. You suffered so much doing good, acting justly, knowing that at the right time it would all work out. You trusted the Father and obeyed him. I really want the same for my life.

Help me not to look for praise or for good to be returned to me. Give me your patience and the reward of knowing you. I want my pleasure to be found in doing your will and knowing your heart. How great it would be to have confidence in one thing—that God knows me, and I know him!

You never tire of doing good, Father. You just don't quit. Thank you for insisting that I am a part of your family. Though I may have given up, you endured. Though I may have been discouraged, you were encouraging. Thank you for your goodness and the promise of your rewards. It helps me to keep going, knowing that you have such great things for me.

Your People

To all who mourn in Israel, he will give a crown of beauty for ashes, a joyous blessing instead of mourning, festive praise instead of despair. In their righteousness, they will be like great oaks that the LORD has planted for his own glory.

ISAIAH 61:3 NLT

Father, you love your people. Thank you for grafting me in with your chosen ones. Though I was a foreigner, you made me like your own. Help me to be a blessing to others as you have blessed me. I know that my righteousness is found in you alone, and I pray for my brothers and sisters around the world that they would know you.

I pray peace for Israel. I pray that each man and woman would know you personally, Jesus. Your love for them is unabashed; it blazes within you. I want to love others in this way.

God, Israel will be redeemed, and joy will replace mourning. You will restore your people to yourself, and I am included! Thank you for saving me and for adopting me into your family.

Stand in Stillness

I am standing in absolute stillness,
silent before the one I love,
waiting as long as it takes for him to rescue me.
Only God is my Savior, and he will not fail me.

PSALM 62:5 TPT

Savior, give me patience. Help me when I am surrounded by my enemies to trust in you. Rescue me and show me the way of escape. I know that I can trust in you, so I speak to my soul and tell it to wait upon you, to be still and know that you are God.

Spirit, help me. Give me your words of truth and strength. I know that my life is found in you and death awaits me outside. I want my life to be buried with you, Christ, that I may be resurrected into a new life with you. Give me the endurance and patience to get there.

I wait upon you, God, and you answer me. You have never failed me. I can trust in you because of your faithfulness and your character. You alone are my salvation.

Humble State

O Lord, you are our Father;
we are the clay, and you are our potter;
we are all the work of your hand.

ISAIAH 64:8 ESV

I am a broken vessel, God, yet you use me to do your work. Thank you for using me despite my standing in this life. I know because I recognize my state, you love to use me. You work with those who are in need and remain humble.

You know me, God, and you are patient with me. Help me to trust in the work you are doing. Forgive me for my haste when I try to do too much without you. Lead me by the still waters and the places of peace. Let me hear you and understand your ways.

What a great Father I have! You are personally involved in my life, which amazes me considering how many people there are for you to love. You are so good at working with me. You are kind, gentle, honest, and caring. Your strength is my power, and your love is my passion. You keep me going.

For Me

"As a mother comforts her child,
so I will comfort you."

Isaiah 66:13 niv

Lord, I need your strength today. I have mountains to climb.
I don't even know where to start with all that I have going
on. Please bring clarity to my mind and lift me out of this
quagmire of indecision. Guide me to your truth and give me
friends that speak light and life into my situation. Surround
me with sound wisdom that comes from your Spirit.

Holy Spirit, comfort me in my trouble and help me make
sense of my life. I don't want to lose the momentum I have
with you. Don't leave me or pass me by; rather, fill me
afresh today.

*God, you are a refreshing stream on a hot day, a cool
shower in a dry desert. Thank you for your comfort,
strength, and guidance. I trust in you to lead me on the right
path. Thank you for answering my prayers and comforting
me. I know that you are for me and not against me.*

Helper and Defender

Father to the fatherless, defender of widows—
this is God, whose dwelling is holy.

PSALM 68:5 NLT

Lord, give me a passion to do the things you want to do on earth. I ask that your will would be done here as it is in heaven. Jesus, I am willing to do what you want. Help me to know the way to do things. If left in my hands, I fear I may hurt someone or take things too far.

You know my weakness and my pent-up frustrations with the wickedness of this world. It is all so broken, God. Remove the man who harms orphans and children. Destroy the man who harms the widow. Give me your heart to help those in need.

Thank you for your protection over those who have none, Father. You desire to save all men, and you have saved me. Thank you for your salvation. Continue to speak through me to others. Your Spirit is a witness with my spirit that you are actively working within all men to know you and your salvation.

The Lowest Point

The humble will see their God at work and be glad.
Let all who seek God's help be encouraged.

PSALM 69:32 NLT

Father, we both know how broken men are. I am humbled by your graciousness toward me. Help me to encourage those around me who seek you humbly. Give me the words to remind others about how good you are to those in need.

Help me, with your strength, to rebuke the prideful, and to encourage all men to submit their lives to you. Work in me, so others see what your love and fruit look like in a man. I want to be like you, Jesus, loving others even unto death.

Father, you reward the humble by lifting them up. Your Son was glorified above all because he humbled himself to the lowest point. You are faithful to bring joy to those who mourn and to make those righteous who grieve their sin. You are the God of compassion and kindness.

December

The Lord is close to everyone
who prays to him,
to all who truly pray to him.

Psalm 145:18 NCV

Heal the Land

"If My people who are called by My name humble themselves and pray and seek My face and turn from their wicked ways, then I will hear from heaven, will forgive their sin and will heal their land."

2 CHRONICLES 7:14 ESV

Father, please heal our land. We are a perverse and sinful people, and we desperately need you to come remove our sin. We are guilty of murdering thousands of babies, placing the poor in bondage, taking advantage of the needy, and being unjust. You hate our deceit and pride.

Forgive us, Lord. I pray that you would awaken your Church. Engage us with your Spirit and pour out on us a fresh anointing. Help us to live holy lives that exemplify and honor you. Turn our hearts away from evil and make us a Church that is pleasing to you.

God, you are generous and giving. You are willing to forgive all who seek you. There is no question about the joy you give to those who humble themselves. You will hear us, forgive us, and cleanse our land.

That Great Day

"The Lamb in the midst of the throne will be their shepherd, and he will guide them to springs of living water, and God will wipe away every tear from their eyes."

REVELATION 7:17 ESV

Jesus, you are on your way back! Thank you for the hope this gives me in the midst of this life. I need to be encouraged that you will come back and make things right. Help me to be ready for your return. Prepare my heart. Where the soil is hard, tear it up. Show me areas of sin, unforgiveness, or the parts covered in shame.

I want all of my life to be yours. I want you to be glorified in me. Father, all the tears I have cried, all the anger and pain I have felt, all the sickness in my body, wash it all away by your blood.

Father, your words comfort my soul. I know that one day I will stand with you in your victory of sin and death. I will rise with you and enter into my inheritance. God, I so look forward to this great day!

Never Let Go

Once again you will have compassion on us.
You will trample our sins under your feet
and throw them into the depths of the ocean!

MICAH 7:19 NLT

Father, my heart is tenderized by your incessant knocking.
Thank you for never letting me go. I was hard of heart and
head, but you found a way by your Spirit to break through.
I agree with you, I open the door of my heart.

Help me today to remain steadfast in letting you in. I ask
that you would protect what we have. I pray you would
guard my heart with me. Help me to see where the enemy
wants to get in and place double protection over those
areas in which I am vulnerable.

*God, thank you for your compassion and kindness that
leads me to repentance. Because of your mercy I am
forever yours. My sin is covered, and my shame has been
taken away. You have my loyalty. You are my rock and my
fortress. By your grace, I will follow you the rest of my life.*

Praying for Me

He is able, once and forever, to save those who come to God through him. He lives forever to intercede with God on their behalf.

HEBREWS 7:25 NLT

Jesus, after all you have done for me, it is amazing to think that you continue by interceding for me. It is such a gift to know this, and it inspires me to be the same for those around me—even for those who sin against me. Help me to love in a manner that will enable me to pray for my enemies.

I pray that my life will be filled with your passion and energy to engage people in a discussion about you. I want them to know the salvation that I know. Give me your boldness to share the truth and speak with love.

Thank you, Christ, for your liberty. You have provided freedom to me, and I believe in you. Your prayers for me give me strength, and I trust that you have the best in mind for me. I surrender myself to your will because you are perfect in your leadership.

Open Door

"Ask and it will be given to you; seek and you will find;
knock and the door will be opened to you."

MATTHEW 7:7 NIV

Thank you, God, that you are not a liar. You do not promote something then take it away. I am asking that you would help me to be more like you in all things. I know that you want me to live a righteous life, and I want this too.

Help me to seek you, because as I do, I will find you, and then I will walk as you walked. I can see how it should play out in my life, but I fail to execute the plan. I am asking, I am seeking, and I am knocking. My door is open for you to come in and make changes. I pray that you would act quickly on my behalf.

Thank you that you answer those who knock. You open the door with a warm smile and welcoming arms. I believe that you allow those who seek you to find you. You are not one to stay hidden. You want me to know you. I also trust that what I ask will be given to me according to your will.

Best Intentions

"Know therefore that the LORD your God is God; he
is the faithful God, keeping his covenant of love to a
thousand generations of those who love him and keep
his commandments."

DEUTERONOMY 7:9 NIV

Faithful God, please continue to be patient with me as I
grow in you. You know my path and the direction of my
heart. I seek after you with the best intentions but so often
I fail to remain faithful like you.

Help me to do all that you ask of me and remain upright in
my walk with you. Help me to remain steadfast in my walk
and give me the joy and endurance I need to love you with
all my heart.

*You are my Lord and Savior. I will follow you to the ends of
the earth because you continue to uphold me. At your right
hand my enemies are cut off, and I have victory with you.
I know that your love will never fail me or keep me from
entering into your promises.*

Made Holy

There is therefore now no condemnation
for those who are in Christ Jesus.

ROMANS 8:1 ESV

Father, I know in my heart that when I do wrong, I want
to condemn myself. I want to punish myself somehow
or redeem myself by doing good. Thank you for your
forgiveness. I receive it.

I want to walk in the freedom of your forgiveness and
mercy. Not so I can sin more, but so I find new energy and
enthusiasm for righteousness. I need you, Holy Spirit, to fill
me with a hunger for doing what is right. Help me to follow
after you and obey you.

*God, you have forgiven me before I even sinned. You
only ask that I come humbly before you and accept your
sacrifice as atonement for my sin. I have no condemnation
in you but am set apart; I am made holy by your actions. I
find liberty in you and comfort from your Holy Spirit.*

Alluring Light

"I am the light of the world.
Whoever follows me will not walk in darkness,
but will have the light of life."

JOHN 8:12 ESV

What is it about light that is so alluring? The sun, moon, and stars catch my eyes all the time. Bright, flickering lights distract me at night. You, Jesus, are that light that I want to be distracted by.

Help me to be caught up with you, and when I am not, flicker at me, shine on me, and light up my path. You guide me by your truth and through your Holy Spirit. I ask that my heart would be fully engaged with you so I will never leave your path of righteousness.

God, in you I have life and liberty. I am not deceived or in darkness, but I walk in the truth and the light. You have freed me from sin, and I am fully aware of your goodness and love for me. Continue your strengthening work in my heart as you pour out your Spirit upon me.

Abba

You have not received a spirit that makes you fearful slaves. Instead, you received God's Spirit when he adopted you as his own children. Now we call him, "Abba, Father."

ROMANS 8:15 NLT

Father, I do not fear like a man enslaved, but I do revere you. I respect you as my authority, and I pray that would be evidenced in my obedience to your Word. Help me to show others how much I love you.

I know you make it clear it is those who obey you who love you. I want to obey. Help me in my unbelief. Give me a heart that is tender to you and sensitive to your Spirit. Show me, as your child, the good things that you have for me and how much you take care of me.

God, you are a good father. You give gifts that enable me to be competent, equipped, and effective. I am your son, and as such, you take care of all my needs. You store up for me an inheritance which will never perish, spoil, or fade. Thank you for your kindness, patience, and mercy.

The Difference

I will show my love to those who passionately love me.
For they will search and search continually
until they find me.

PROVERBS 8:17 TPT

Help me to not stop seeking you, God. It is easy to be distracted by this life. I have so many opportunities with jobs, people, and media, to lose sight of you. I want my life to be a continual pursuit of you and the things you love.

Help me to differentiate between what you love and what I desire. Give me your desires as I learn to delight in you. Show me your ways and help me, Holy Spirit, to be guided into your truth and light.

Father, you love those who seek you. You are the rewarder of the diligent. Those who are meek and seek will find and inherit the earth. You are helping me to find you, and you are leading me to yourself. I am thankful for your guidance and your encouragement. You are such a good father, and I trust in your leadership and love.

Once Again

He will once again fill your mouth with laughter
and your lips with shouts of joy.

JOB 8:21 NLT

Jesus, I ask that you would help me to fill my mind and
heart with the right things. I can easily be entertained
by the offerings of this life and forget what is truly
important—a heart devoted to you.

I know that when I am tuned in to you, my heart is at its
happiest and I am full of joy. I pray you would continue to
develop me into the man who demonstrates your character
and love for others. I ask that you would help me get to the
day when there will be no more tears and only joy.

*You delight in me, Father. You share that delight in the
presence of your Spirit, who dwells with me and fills me
with joy and peace that lasts forever. I am secure in you,
and I can know your pleasure for me. I will continue to trust
in your goodness and the strength of your character.*

Help in Weakness

The Spirit helps us with our weakness. We do not know how to pray as we should. But the Spirit himself speaks to God for us, even begs God for us with deep feelings that words cannot explain.

ROMANS 8:26 NCV

Holy Spirit, please continue to help me pray. Remind me to be present with you and to reflect upon the glory and majesty of Jesus. I know that you want me to hear you and follow your leading. I pray that you would guide me in the right ways and increase my pleasure in you. I want my heart to be joined to yours as we dwell together on this earth.

I want to accomplish your work, Jesus, and be a pleasing servant. Help me to pray these things. Speak for me to the Father. Fill my mouth with your words.

God, thank you for sending the Holy Spirit to be a helper to me. Holy Spirit, you guide me in the truth and lead me. I will trust in you to bring me into my final resting place in Christ. You are my assurance of the resurrection.

Sole Craving

We know that for those who love God all things work together for good, for those who are called according to his purpose.

ROMANS 8:28 ESV

Lord, I love you. I pray for my heart, my will, and my emotions, that they would be fully yours. I desire for my life to be devoted to the pursuit of you and that my deepest intentions would drive me to you.

I want you to be the sole craving of my soul. In my mind I know that when I take delight in you, I will pray what you pray, and I will walk as you want me to walk. Fill me with a passion for your calling and lead me in your purposes.

God, you are faithful to complete the good work in me that you began long ago. I will trust in your character and leadership, and I will lean on you and not on my own understanding. You continue to give me your Spirit who strengthens and enables me to do your will. I will listen to you, Holy Spirit, and be led by you according to God's will.

Dwell in Peace

Jesus said to the Jews who had believed him, "If you abide in my word, you are truly my disciples, and you will know the truth, and the truth will set you free."

JOHN 8:31-32 ESV

Jesus, help me to know your truth and abide in you. I don't want to ever leave you or forsake you. Help my heart to be devoted to you alone.

I want to know what it means to rest in you and not fight with your Spirit. I pray that my home would be with you where we dwell together in peace. Your Word fills my heart with joy. I love to obey you and do the things you ask of me.

Jesus, I believe in you. I am your disciple because your Spirit dwells in me, and the truth of your Word bears witness in my heart to my adoption as a son of God. Thank you for setting me free with your truth and the realization that I am your child.

Loving Life

> "If you try to hang on to your life, you will lose it. But if you give up your life for my sake and for the sake of the Good News, you will save it. And what do you benefit if you gain the whole world but lose your own soul?"
>
> MARK 8:35-36 NLT

Father, I do love life. I believe you put that in all of us. I was never designed to die, and I believe I will live forever because of you. But I know what you are saying here: that I would not hold on to the things of this life.

Help me not to love mammon, but to turn my whole heart to you. Help me to serve you and no other god. I want to be willing to lay down my life in obedience to you.

God, you are my provider, and I can trust in your care of me. You also guide me and protect me from those who wish to do me harm. You have saved me from sin and death, and I will be resurrected to be with you again. My life is yours.

What I Need

Even in the midst of all these things, we triumph
over them all, for God has made us to be more than
conquerors, and his demonstrated love is our glorious
victory over everything.

ROMANS 8:37 TPT

My heart is weak at times, Jesus. I don't want to face
adversity and fail. I want to be an overcomer. I pray that
you would save me from becoming cynical and jaded by
life. It can be wearying facing the woes of the world and
not seeing any progress in your kingdom.

Save me from falling away from you because of my
offense. Lift my eyes to you and help me to recollect your
promises and your victories. You are what I need right now.

*You are the greatest. You are my God, and you are
victorious. You have overcome death and sin, and Satan will
be vanquished forever when you come and judge all things.
My life is sheltered in you, and I experience the joy of your
salvation because you are my covering.*

Convinced

I am convinced that neither death nor life, neither angels nor demons, neither the present nor the future, nor any powers, neither height nor depth, nor anything else in all creation, will be able to separate us from the love of God that is in Christ Jesus our Lord.

ROMANS 8:38-39 NIV

I am so pleased that I am in your kingdom, Father. Fill my heart with the joy of your salvation. Help me to see your love and feel it active in my life.

In my head I know this word, but sometimes my heart drifts far from the truth of it. You are my source and my future. Help me to rest in the knowledge of your care for me.

There is no other god. You alone are God. I can trust in you and your enduring love. Your faithfulness does not end. You are committed to me like no other person, and I love how convinced I am of your care.

Thick and Thin

The LORD God is like a sun and shield;
the LORD gives us kindness and honor.
He does not hold back anything good
from those whose lives are innocent.

PSALM 84:11 NCV

Wow, God. You know my heart is not innocent, but I know that you have cleansed me of all sin because of what Christ has done for me. Encourage me in this. Help me to hold on to the promises I have in you.

At times I can be afraid of my own fragility, yet you seem to come alongside me and give me hope. Holy Spirit, do not pass me by. Stay with me and remind me of God's goodness.

Father, you have purified my heart and made me clean before you. Jesus, thank you so much for your salvation and Holy Spirit, thank you for your sanctifying work in me. I love that you stick with me through thick and thin.

Draped in Love

How enriched are they
who find their strength in the Lord;
within their hearts are the highways of holiness!

PSALM 84:5 TPT

You are all that I need, God. I keep telling myself this over and over again. Drum it into me, so I am not dependent on any other. I believe you can make me a better man if you can help me to accept who I am and I can live according to your Word.

I will know your strength when I can fully lean upon you. That is what I want to learn to do. You know it is not easy for me. I am a confident man, capable in many ways. You have made me like this, but despite that, you call for me to depend upon you. Help me, Jesus!

You are holy. There is none like my God! You are beautiful and powerful. Magnificent and gentle. Such a dichotomy of wonderful things. There is no evil in you though. I understand this truth. All you do is draped in love, and you are consistent in demonstrating this.

Record Removed

You, O LORD, are good and forgiving,
abounding in steadfast love to all who call upon you.

PSALM 86:5 ESV

I am amazed by your goodness, God. Help me to
be consistent like you. I want to show kindness and
forgiveness to others like you show to me. Increase my
faith to believe that you will give me the strength to love
others and show mercy like you do.

I want to know your joy in the midst of suffering and your
comfort when I am troubled. Fill me, Holy Spirit, with your
understanding of Christ, and strengthen me as you did him
when he walked the earth.

*Father, you are good to me. You shower me with mercy
and love. Your forgiveness removes the record of all my
wrongs. You have loved me and continue to do so despite
my inadequacies. Thank you for your faithfulness in being
present in my life at all times.*

Grace Always

I will be strength to him
and I will give him my grace
to sustain him no matter what comes.

PSALM 89:21 TPT

Lord, there are many things that try to entrap me. Some people I come across want to see me fail or want to use me for their own desires, but you have protected me and given me ways to escape. I need you to continue to do this in me.

Help me, God, to remain steadfast in serving you and showing others what it means to be a man of grace. I want them to see, despite my failures, how much you love me and continue to use me.

God, you are my refuge. You are the warrior who fights my battles and helps me escape the enemy. You protect my soul and set a rampart around me. I know I am confident because of you; my heart is content and ready to serve because of your great faithfulness.

Never Forsaken

Those who know your name trust in you,
for you, Lord, have never forsaken those who seek you.

PSALM 9:10 NIV

There are times when my heart is far from you, Jesus. I am sorry that I allow it to become that way. I feel ashamed because of it especially when I compare myself to your faithfulness. You are such a rock to me, yet I seem so flippant in comparison.

I pray I would grow in my trust of you and my faithfulness toward you. I know what I want in my heart, but I am troubled by the worries of life and the enticements it offers to alleviate anxiety. Help me, Holy Spirit, to be faithful.

God, you are trustworthy and true. You are a storehouse of strength compared to my walk of weakness. In you alone I have all I need to be faithful and follow in your footsteps. I trust in you, Jesus. I know you will not forsake me even in my lowest state. You will be there when I need you.

With One Word

"Everything is possible
for one who believes."

MARK 9:23 NIV

I have read this so many times and thought what do I
believe that could become possible? Help me, Jesus, not
to limit you because of my lack of faith. Draw me so close
that when you speak something, I act and see it come to
fruition.

I want my thoughts to be yours and my will to follow after
yours. Come and do on the earth what you do in heaven
and reestablish yourself as the preeminent being of all your
creation. I long for you to come back and make things right.

*Jesus, you created the world with your word. You are the
Word of God, and all things began through you. In you and
through you I have my existence. Through your Word alone
all things will come to pass as you destined them to. Your
Word is true and does not return void; it will always bear
fruit in my life and in this world.*

Deity to Babe

To us a child is born,
To us a son is given;
and the government shall be upon his shoulder,
and his name shall be called
Wonderful Counselor, Mighty God,
Everlasting Father, Prince of Peace.

ISAIAH 9:6 ESV

Jesus, you are my light and my salvation. I pray that you would be glorified in my life. Help me to embrace humility like you did from a deity to babe. Show me the ways I resist walking as you did. Help me, through your Spirit, to recognize and change those things in me that do not align with your principles.

You showed the way, giving everything to accomplish the will of the Father. I ask that you would do this in me as well.

You are glorified, Christ. You are lifted high, and I bow my knee before you. King of kings and Lord of lords, you are exceptional—set apart from all men. I worship you alone; you are seated at the right hand of the Father. Your kingdom is eternal; it dwells with me in my heart forever.

In Abundance

God is able to provide you
with every blessing in abundance,
so that by always having enough of everything,
you may share abundantly in every good work.

2 Corinthians 9:8 NRSV

Help me to give as you have given. You do not hold
anything back for my success including your own life,
Jesus. Show me how to walk in a similar manner. I want
you to be glorified in me as I complete your will. I want to
be able to trust in you to provide everything, so I willingly
share with others.

When I don't trust in you, I tend to want to horde things and
make sure I am taken care of. Break me free from this, so I
can store up treasures in heaven rather than here on earth.

*God, you are my eternal security. You have given all for
the benefit of others. You gave your Son to us. Jesus, you
humbled yourself to the lowest extent becoming like the rest
of your creation. Thank you, Holy Spirit, for dwelling with a
broken vessel like me to sanctify and make me like Christ.*

Established

The LORD is a refuge for the oppressed,
a stronghold in times of trouble.

PSALM 9:9 NIV

Help me when I am in trouble to run to you, God. I pray that my mind would be sanctified and set apart for you. When I face temptation or trial, let me be reminded of your great promises. Holy Spirit, whisper in my ear in the quiet times, and shout at me when I need it. I pray for your continued presence in my life, so I would not depart from doing your will.

So many times, I have found myself in trouble, and you have rescued me. Eventually I end up turning to you; I just pray that it will be quicker each time.

I am not alone because I am surrounded by your angels and full of your Spirit. Thank you, Jesus, for always being with me through good and bad times. Your presence is exactly what I need each time, and I will run to you for protection and security. You have established me as your child.

Good Gardener

Those who live in the shelter of the Most High
will find rest in the shadow of the Almighty.

PSALM 91:1 NLT

It is always my intention to find you in the middle of my
trouble, God. My heart longs for you to rescue me from
turmoil, but so often it seems you are far from me. Please
show me yourself when I am struggling to see my way out
of a bad situation. I don't want to be left floundering in my
trouble.

Show me how you are giving me strength and sheltering
me from the dangers that seem to be overwhelming. I want
to abide in you always.

*Father, you are the true vine, and I am the branch. I see
how you are pruning me to bring greater growth in my life.
I trust in you as the good gardener. You keep the birds and
pests away that trouble me. I know you are producing in
me good fruit and I will trust in your protection. Continue
your good work in me, Jesus.*

At Your Feet

The LORD says, "I will rescue those who love me.
I will protect those who trust in my name."

PSALM 91:14 NLT

Father, I lay myself at your feet. I ask that you would show me your kindness and take me, the stranger, into your home. Feed me and clothe me. Protect me from the elements of life and the wickedness of the world.

I pray for your continued favor. Show me your ways and lead me on paths that take me to you. I don't want my heart to be led astray, even by supposedly good things on the side of the road that may distract me. Make my path straight and my foot secure.

God, you are my guide and my helper. I am never lost or troubled because you are by my side. In you I am sure of my path and my lot is secure. I have before me a clear direction—a successful path to salvation. I am saved by grace and made holy by your sanctification. Thank you for my assurance and for the presence of your Sprit within me.

Empowering Grace

I will say of the LORD,
"He is my refuge and my fortress;
My God, in Him I will trust."

PSALM 91:2 NKJV

I have told people to trust me, and others have asked me to trust them. Jesus, I want to pledge my trust to you. Help me in this, as you know how fickle I am. One day I can say this, and the next I am relying on myself. I want to lay myself at your feet again and ask that you would forgive me for making so much of life about me.

Thank you for your forgiveness and your empowering grace. I will take hold of your mercy and rely on you to change me. Father, make me more like your Son.

God, you do not need me, but you want me. How awesome it is to be desired by you! I will return this passion. I will pursue you and love you. I can do so because of your work in me. You have secured me with the presence of your Spirit. He helps and teaches me all things.

Hidden Securely

He will cover you with his feathers.
He will shelter you with his wings.
His faithful promises are your armor and protection.

PSALM 91:4 NLT

God, help me to follow you. I want my life to be a discovery of the good things I have in you. Out of these, I want to be a witness for you. Hide my life so securely in you that all others see is you. I know you want to do great things through me, so you are glorified.

Holy Spirit, fill me with your love, the truth of your Word, and the power of your resurrection. Cocoon me so I can change and be more like you. As I emerge, let others see the beauty you have created in me.

Father, I know you want me to be part of your gathering at the end of the age. You have stored up great things for me. I trust that your protection and promises will endure. I will be with you at the end of the age.

Joyfully Content

When anxiety was great within me,
your consolation brought me joy.

Psalm 94:19 niv

Father, I need you more than I know. I delight in you, and I want to do so more. Help me to turn my heart to you even in the most troubled times. Life can get to me quickly; anxieties overwhelm me, but I know you can draw me out of them and give me the strength I need to endure.

Holy Spirit, show me when you are doing this so I can be encouraged and know your closeness. I want my life to be content because of you and no other. I want to be full of your joy because I know that it will endure forever!

You are my comfort, Holy Spirit. Because of you I have great joy that will last forever. I am certain of my salvation because of your presence in my life. I know you will never leave or forsake me. Because of this, my life is joyfully content.